A HOUSE UNITED

A HOUSE UNITED

How the Church Can Save the World

Allen Hilton

Fortress Press

Minneapolis

CONTENTS

INTRODUCTION

Dietrich Bonhoeffer loved his time in London. At the invitation of a friend, the young German churchman, who would twelve years later die a martyr during the last days of Nazi control, had taken a post across the English Channel. Bonhoeffer had signed on to serve two small German-speaking churches, where he preached, taught, visited the sick, cared for the elderly, and otherwise lived out the role of a pastor to his small urban parishes. These were holy projects, and the young Rev. Dr. Bonhoeffer took them on with his customary intensity and devotion. He felt as if he were doing well.

Despite Bonhoeffer's ministerial success, his mentor and friend Karl Barth had clearly had enough of his protégé's sojourn in England. Bonhoeffer had written to Barth about "the calm of the parish ministry" and other pleasant aspects of his work that in other times would have pleased Barth. But in 1933, they did not. From the cauldron of his own work opposing the Third Reich and his academic post in

Bonn, Barth shot Bonhoeffer a terse, apocalyptic-sounding letter: "You are a German, . . . the house of your church is on fire, . . . you must return to your post by the next ship."[1] For Barth, Bonhoeffer's English sojourn would have been fine at other times, but at that moment, a much more urgent and significant need beckoned: "Your house is on fire!"

Like Bonhoeffer in London, Christian churches in the United States are doing many good things. Some are creating innovative forms of worship; others are stepping out into new ways of forming the lives in their care. Many tend well to their sick and elderly. Mission work also continues apace, as churches I know dispatch members to Haiti, Kenya, Nicaragua, Mexico, Saint Thomas, and a host of other international places of need. Other good churches reach to communities in dire straits closer to home. Some advocate for justice in their cities. Others spread the word of the gospel to neighbors who have not yet embraced it. Still others work to secure religious liberty in their lands. A lot of churches are doing a lot of good things.

But for all our good and faithful labor in God's vineyard, if Karl Barth were alive today, I think he'd write the churches in the United States a strongly worded note: "You're American, . . . your nation's house is on fire, . . . turn around and put it out!"

There has been literal fire, to be sure. After the 2016 presidential election, conflagrations in downtown Portland, Oregon, and Akron, Ohio, vented protestors' anger.[2] But the American burn has spread far beyond those few small street fires. It has singed families, friendships, corporations, schools, sports teams, and almost every other community among us.

If I were to stop here and let the American people guess what this menacing fire might be, I'd get two main answers. Half of the nation would say, "The problem is those blasted liberals. They want to dole out our dollars to lazy people, siphon the energy out of our economy with regulations, promote atheism by taking Christianity out of everything, and reduce sexuality to an opinion." Asked the same question, the other half of the country would say, "It's those damned conservatives! They want to shrink government just small enough to fit in our bedrooms, they don't care about the poor or the helpless, they go to war for sport, and they oppress brown-skinned people." Anger would escalate on both sides and soon become a brawl.

The American church has bought into that definition of the fire. Christian leaders and churches identify with blue or red, imagining that righteous political convictions license us to nurse open disdain for half the nation. When the country elected Barack

Obama in 2008, pastors on the Right declared war against his coming attack on the very existence of Christianity. When Donald Trump took office in January 2017, leaders on the Left gathered their troops to join the Resistance and oppose all things Trump, whose (to their eyes) blatant racism, sexism, and American isolationism would, by their light, doom the land.

If Karl Barth were to pen a strongly worded letter to us, I don't imagine he would find the offending fire in the Left or the Right, in progressive Christians or conservative Christians. Rather, Barth would call us to extinguish the disunion itself—division that has turned college campuses into war zones, disabled our government, and given us enemies in our own towns. Polarization numbers have risen to levels unseen since the Civil War and now threaten even to surpass those. The Left-Right line divides urban from rural, educated from uneducated, working class from professional class, and so on and so on. Maybe even more personally jarring is the way it has broken families and friendships. One tribe doesn't just disagree with the other, it fears them.

But you really don't need me to describe our division. You know it well, because it has become the way of life in our land. It's the water we swim in—so much so that we no longer even pay lip service to becoming "a more perfect union." *Time* magazine's 2016 Person of the Year cover surprised no one when it characterized its recipient as "Donald J. Trump, President of the Divided States of America." Our rift has made us meaner. It has disengaged us from one another in ways that leave us confounded before our political opposites. As one author has put it, "Intellectually and emotionally weakened by years of steadily degraded public discourse, we are now two separate ideological countries, LeftLand and RightLand, speaking different languages, the lines between us down."[3]

In the face of our debilitating division, a wise Christian elder of the early twenty-first century would grab the American church by the shirt collar and say, "Your nation's house is on fire! Your communities and your civility are nearly consumed. It's time to get your gear on and grab a hose!" In fact, that's exactly what I'm saying.

At this point, you may feel tempted to put the book down and stop reading. You didn't sign up for sirens or screed. Maybe the subtitle, "How the Church Can Save the World," piqued your interest. God built the church to save the world, after all, and if God is calling us to a new way to do that, you're in. You feel the brokenness around you, and you're looking for ways to help heal it. You're already on board, and you don't want to be scolded. If this description fits you, maybe a pastoral letter from the prophet Jeremiah to Israel's exiles will sit better than Karl Barth's harangue. Okay, then let's go there.

Twenty-six centuries ago, King Nebuchadnezzar of Babylon destroyed Jerusalem, and his soldiers force-marched the people of that city and its Judean surroundings toward present-day Iraq. But Jeremiah stayed behind in Jerusalem. At a distance, sitting amid the ashes of a once-proud city, the weeping prophet counseled his people on life in their new city. Exile had left them angry and confused, consigned to the province of foreign gods, foreign customs, foreign language, and foreign food. One of their poets sang out their collective anguish, "How can we sing the Lord's song in a foreign land?" (Psalm 137:4).

Jeremiah's response surely surprised them if they expected to hear a prophet's righteous condemnation of all things Babylonian. Jeremiah went the other way, and his words to those ancient exiles move across the ages and land in our twenty-first-century laps:

Thus says the Lord of hosts, the God of Israel, to all the exiles whom I have sent into exile from Jerusalem to Babylon: "Build houses and

live in them; plant gardens and eat what they
produce. . . . Seek the welfare of the city where
I have sent you into exile, and pray to the Lord
on its behalf, for in its welfare you will find your
welfare." (Jeremiah 29:4, 7, NIV)

Put down roots, exiles. Dig in and help your new
neighbors.

In every age, God calls Christians (and Jews, too)
to hear and live out these words where we are, to
seek the welfare of our cities. And as we do that,
we ask together what are our land's most pressing
needs—what gift would most help our neighbors in
our time. A wise Christian elder surveying the needs
of our land in the first quarter of the twenty-first
century would put "Help people come together
across difference" on her short list.

Whether you want Karl Barth to grab you by the
scruff or the prophet Jeremiah to coax you to engage,
the message is the same. The hard truths of our present American crisis of polarization are these: The
church is complicit in it, and we must consider why
we've grown so fond of our habit of division (part
1), and that complicit church is called to answer that
polarization with our own mutually-loving alternative (part 2).

The whole hope originates with a little prayer

Jesus spoke with some of his very last words to his disciples:

> My prayer is not for them alone. I pray also for those who will believe in me through their message, that all of them may be one, Father, just as you are in me and I am in you. May they also be in us so that the world may believe that you have sent me. I have given them the glory that you gave me, that they may be one as we are one—I in them and you in me—so that they may be brought to complete unity. Then the world will know that you sent me and have loved them even as you have loved me. (John 17:20–23, NIV)

Becoming the answer to that prayer would bless the church, and it just might save the world.

NOTES

1. Dietrich Bonhoeffer's Works 13 (1/2, 1/16) (London: 1933–1935; Minneapolis: Fortress Press, 2007).

2. "Post-election Protesters March in Portland for Second Night," Fox 12 Oregon, updated November 10, 2016,

https://tinyurl.com/ybzgxnt6; Associated Press, "Witnesses: Man Sets Himself on Fire after Post-election Rant," *Toledo Blade*, November 20, 2016, https://tinyurl.com/y82gw625.

3. George Saunders, "Who Are All These Trump Supporters?," *New Yorker*, July 11–18, 2016, https://tinyurl.com/yayxlkvk.

THE DIVIDED STATES OF AMERICA

A house divided against itself cannot stand.

—Jesus of Nazareth
and Abraham Lincoln of Illinois

On November 9, 2016, three hundred million Americans absorbed what we had done the day before. "We the people" had elected Donald J. Trump to be our forty-fifth president. The campaign that led up to that moment was the most divisive and rhetorically violent in generations. Debates became a farcical race to the bottom. Campaigns went very negative very early, and the ugliness escalated to the bitter end, so that, by Election Day, the two candidates were the least favored pair of party nominees in recorded US history. When news of Donald Trump's victory broke, half of the country could not fathom what the other half had done. Violent protests erupted in cities, while farm towns and outer-ring suburbs rejoiced. Left-wingers mourned the end of civilization as we know it, while many right-wingers celebrated the coming freedom of the market and a train of conservative Supreme Court justices to come. Families split and friendships broke as an already-divided nation had a historically divided day.

Some blamed Trump for causing the division that flared up during the campaign. But anyone who has been watching American politics and culture over the last quarter century should know otherwise: that deep fault lines had begun to divide our nation long before Donald Trump launched his campaign for president, or even his first "Birther" claims against President Obama's legitimate citizenship in 2011. We had seen the polarization statistics rise, had experienced the disintegration of bipartisanship in government and of common-good collaboration in culture. Some analysts had even begun to compare the America they saw around them to the one that had taken up arms to settle the slavery dispute fifteen decades earlier.

In June of 1858, the United States of America were
not very united at all. The union held seventeen free
states and fifteen slave states, and the political chasm
between the two Americas was widening. In that
charged context, Abraham Lincoln found himself in
the middle of a campaign for a US Senate seat in Illinois. As he looked out over the people gathered for
that state's Republican Party convention, his eyes
scanned beyond that room to the nation surrounding it. His speech became famous. The words
he reached for were first uttered by Jesus: "'A house
divided against itself cannot stand.' I believe this
government cannot endure permanently half slave
and half free."[1]

Abraham Lincoln's prophecy came true three
years later, and for the first time in our four-score-
and seven-year history, American soldiers took to
the battlefield against one another.

A SECOND CIVIL WAR?

Just more than 150 years after the last shots were fired
at Appomattox, Americans find ourselves again battling one another. Our warriors don't normally carry
rifles with bayonets, and our warfare does not pit
neatly uniformed soldiers against one another. We
don't wage the battles of this war in grassy fields and

forests, as when the two sides scrimmaged at Gettysburg and Richmond and Bull Run. Though some experienced American diplomats even forecast actual armed civil war to come,[2] and political violence has erupted more frequently of late, we currently fight this war mostly on cable news sets and college campuses, on Twitter feeds and Facebook pages, in churches and Congress and classrooms, and anywhere else Americans disagree on things we're passionate about. This war's opposing colors aren't gray and blue, but red and blue in each state, city, town, neighborhood, and even family.

We called the beginning of our battles "Culture Wars." In his 1991 book of that title, James Davison Hunter named our primary points of conflict—abortion, gun politics, separation of church and state, privacy, recreational drug use, and homosexuality—the frontline issues of our time.[3] A quarter century later, we might add immigration, healthcare, gender identity, and the size and role of government, among others. On these matters, Americans have advanced beyond mere disagreement to a whole new level of enmity. In fact, Hunter summarized the state of American culture at the end of the 2016 political campaigns: "This election brings into relief that America is in some ways two nations within a nation. Each nation has its own values and visions of what the country represents. 'Trump' and 'Clinton' are highly symbolic, like flags around which each nation, or tribe, mobilizes."[4]

Calling these political, racial, and religious disagreements a war may seem overdramatic. After all, people who hope to end poverty, illiteracy, and drugs have called their righteous causes "war" in order to raise the stakes and attract dollars, and in our hype-hungry time, "The War on the Shore" described a Ryder Cup golf match, and the "Cola Wars" pitted Coke versus Pepsi. We overuse that term, so calling the political, religious, and cultural conflicts of our time "war" could be an exaggeration.

That depends on how you define war. The arch-conservative US Supreme Court justice Antonin Scalia died suddenly and unexpectedly in February 2016. Appointed by Ronald Reagan in the 1980s, Scalia—famously or infamously, depending on your perspective—spent his three decades on the bench thundering from the Right on decisions about abortion, same-sex marriage, health care, immigration, campaign finance, and a host of other issues that divide our land. Scalia became a controversial figure, and his decisions evoked vehement response from ideological opponents.

All of this may have looked like politics as usual. But it was not. When people heard of Scalia's death, things got ugly across the aisle. "Dancing on his grave" understates the size and shape of the celebration. In fact, a Twitter meme in the days following his death featured people imagining much more disgusting things to do on that grave.[5] And the partiers were not just extreme, crackpot voices. Prominent public people with many social-media followers —even editors and columnists from mainstream media outlets, including the *New Yorker*, the *Nation*, *Cosmopolitan*, *Vocativ*, *Salon*, and *Rolling Stone*— publicly celebrated with hats and horns.

Similar nastiness naturally comes from the Right, too. At a 2016 campaign rally, conservative commentator Wayne Allyn Root introduced candidate Donald Trump by fantasizing a new made-for-TV movie about Hillary Clinton and her controversial aide, Huma Abedin. Having described a plot in which these two female political renegades drive together across the land spreading mayhem, he painted a gruesome ideal culmination of the plot: "We all get our wish. The ending is like 'Thelma and Louise.'"[6] In other words, a conservative supporter of a Republican presidential candidate publicly relishes the prospect of his Democratic opponent driving off a cliff to her death.

Such unabashed joy at a human death, real or prospective, transported me to other dark historical memories: to May 2, 2011, when Americans danced in the streets after hearing that Osama bin Laden had been killed; and to September 11, 2001, when people danced in Middle Eastern streets as the Twin Towers burned.

The point is, we usually only celebrate the untimely death of a person when she or he is on the opposite side in a war.[7]

BIGOTRY

Let's not stumble on semantics, though. If you don't like the term *war* to describe American polarization, let's use another ugly word: *bigotry*.

In the 1967 film *Guess Who's Coming to Dinner*, Katherine Hepburn and Spencer Tracy play white parents whose daughter has decided to marry a black man, played by Sidney Poitier. Coincidentally, the film appeared the same year that the US Supreme Court struck down anti-miscegenation laws with its decision in *Loving v. Virginia*. American parents were honestly asking, along with Hepburn and Tracy's characters, what they would do if their daughter or son proposed to marry across racial lines.

Sociologists are a clever breed. They probe for social data indirectly, in order not to alarm their subjects into consciousness and a defensive or propriety-focused posture. They won't ask, "Do you hate Muslims?" or "Do you loathe gay people?" or "Do you discriminate against African American people or Mexicans?" People don't answer yes to questions like that. Instead, sociologists might ask a *Guess Who's Coming to Dinner* question: What would you do if your child wanted to marry "one of them"? Now that question no longer works effectively across racial lines. While it sometimes may seem like our culture has not progressed since Tracy and Hepburn posed the question, parents today are much less willing to admit that they'd resist their child's wish to marry across racial lines. "Of course it would be OK!" says even the racist.

Fortunately for sociologists seeking honest answers about American political attitudes, what American legal scholar Cass Sunstein calls "partyism" carries no such stigma. He cites a Stanford-Princeton study titled "Fear and Loathing across Party Lines," which observes, "Americans increasingly dislike people and groups on the other side of the political divide and *face no social repercussions for the open expression of these attitudes.*"[8] For almost six decades, pollsters have been asking Americans, "Would you be displeased if your son or daughter married someone from the opposite political party?" In 1960, on the back end of the 1950s, wearing Donna

Reed sweaters and gray flannel suits and worried about Sputnik, Americans didn't fret much over party lines: 4.5 percent of American respondents answered, "Yes." Five decades later, though, in 2010, when researchers asked Democratic and Republican parents to imagine their offspring's cross-party marriage, that number had risen to 43 percent.[9] We'll explore the reasons for that startling jump later. For now, let's just absorb it: almost half of our nation's parents get the willies when they imagine raising a glass to toast their child's wedded bliss if it means having Damned Democrats or Repulsive Republicans as in-laws.

This may sound absurd, but even amid a resurgence of overt racial hate speech and the alt-right in the US, partyism has surpassed racism among our prejudices. Two Stanford social scientists presented two thousand research subjects with word-association options to reveal their attitude toward people in their own political party versus people from the other. The results indicate strong partisan identity and even stronger suspicion of political opposites. Conservatives couldn't bear to hold "joy" and "Democrat" in their mind at the same time, and progressives balked when asked to let "happy" share their frontal lobe with "Republican."

These prejudiced attitudes will eventually out in

behaviors, such as hiring employees. Companies naturally set out to choose the most qualified candidate to fill every position. So when the Stanford team asked over a thousand subjects to act as employers and weigh two candidates for a job opening, the researchers gave the fictional applicants equivalent skills and qualifications for the positions. But they also snuck subtle clues into the candidates' résumés that would hint at racial identity or political affiliation. As the subjects evaluated candidates, it turned out that race mattered (60 percent of the subjects chose candidates who were from their own race), but politics mattered even more (would-be employers chose their in-party applicant 80 percent of the time).[10] We hire our own, and in the United States right now, political identity has surpassed even race to become the primary definer of "our people."[11] Americans' identities are increasingly tied to our political beliefs.[12]

I'll let you sort out whether it constitutes bigotry to fear that your daughter will marry a certain sort of person, to be unable to hold a specific group and a positive thought on the same frontal lobe, or to be unwilling to hire "one of them" to work at your company.

SEGREGATION

In his book, *The Big Sort,* former *Austin American-Statesman* columnist Bill Bishop reports that Americans increasingly choose to live among our own political tribes. Bishop has scoured census reports and other evidence describing American relocation habits, and it turns out that blue seeks blue and red seeks red: "The Big Sort . . . is the way Americans have chosen to live, an unconscious decision to cluster in communities of like-mindedness."[13]

The US political map increasingly features not just blue and red states, but blue and red neighborhoods. In 1976, less than a quarter (23 percent) of all Americans lived in voting districts where the presidential election was won by a landslide. By 2004, that number had risen to nearly half (47 percent), and the trend has continued. Some will attribute this to partisan gerrymandering, but the book makes it clear that our house-hunting habits have made that grab easier. The Big Sort has a natural logic to it. Bishop writes, "As people seek out the social settings they prefer . . . the nation grows more politically segregated—and the benefit that ought to come with having a variety of opinions is lost to the righteousness that is the special entitlement of homogeneous groups."[14] The title of Bishop's first chapter captures the ethos: "The Age of Political Segregation."

The word *segregation* immediately summons for many of us black-and-white Jim Crow images—separate-but-equal days of yore, with Whites Only signs on drinking fountains and at lunch counters, and National Guardsmen escorting black students into previously all-white Little Rock schools. African Americans certainly didn't choose that kind of segregation. They had little choice. But in our time, at least for those whose means allow them to choose where they live, political segregation is an option, and Americans are choosing it.

Some analysts have updated Mr. Bishop's claims in light of the 2016 presidential election, tracking rural-suburban versus urban voting patterns. They observe that "the widening political divergence between cities and small-town America also reflects a growing alienation between the two groups, and a sense—perhaps accurate—that their fates are not connected." Rural interviewees perceive considerable urban bigotry toward them. A woman from rural Wisconsin says, "The real kicker is that people in the city don't understand us. . . . They don't understand what rural life is like, what's important to us and what challenges that we're facing. They think we're a bunch of redneck racists."[15]

For their part, urbanites also feel misunderstood and resent being depicted by their rural counterparts as either corporate elites or the undeserving poor. Ethnic minorities especially perceive a double standard and feel misunderstood in the widespread white, rural distinction between the deserving and undeserving poor. For example, during the 2016 election season, "almost two-thirds of Trump voters said that average Americans aren't getting as much as they deserve; only 12 percent of Trump supporters said blacks have gotten less than they deserve."[16] These judgments, launched from a distance, widen the chasm.

The rural-versus-urban divide is growing. In one of his first post-election columns in November of 2016, *New York Times* columnist Charles Blow said of the rural-urban divide, "We are living in two diverging Americas at odds and at battle."[17] This sort of segregation builds on itself. Our politics influence our choice of neighborhood, and then our experience of our neighbors affects our choice of politics.[18] And so the cycle continues.

THE DYNAMICS OF POLARIZATION

In the spring of 2016, as North Carolina passed a law that required transgender persons to use bathrooms of the gender assigned to them at birth, protestors from around the nation boycotted the state. Musical artists including Pearl Jam, Bruce Springsteen, and Ringo Starr canceled concerts in North Carolina. Businesses including Deutsche Bank and PayPal put corporate expansion plans on hold. And other state governments prohibited the schools they fund from playing in national championships held in North Carolina.[19]

As that drama played out, a woman's car broke down near Asheville, North Carolina, so she called Shupee Max Towing. When the tow-truck driver arrived, he refused to offer her his service because her car sported a bumper sticker supporting Democratic candidate Bernie Sanders. "I couldn't tow her car because she was obviously a socialist," Mr. Shupe reported. "And when I got in my truck, you know, I was so proud, because I felt like I finally drew a line in the sand and stood up for what I believed."[20]

Progressive America won't play with (or for) Conservative America, and Conservative America won't tow Progressive America. Republican leadership won't fill a Supreme Court seat for a Democratic president, and Democratic representatives in Congress resort to a sit-in on the floor of the House. Polarization stops us in our tracks. It tears the fabric of community, curtailing and even eliminating collaboration and community across difference. Gone are the days of Lincoln's "Team of Rivals," which brought disparate voices into conversation for the country's good, or even the days when Republican president Ronald Reagan and Democratic congressman Tip O'Neill struck deals across the aisle. Across this present divide, compromise is anathema.

Abraham Lincoln looked out at the United States in 1858 and saw "a house divided," and that phrase surely captures our current political culture. The depth of our division is increasing. We have adjusted to a perpetual state of division, and the escalating cruelty of that concession is something our culture has absorbed over time. If the 2016 election season woke many to the extent of it, that new awareness has not turned Americans toward one another. In fact, the political aisle keeps getting wider.

Sociologists who have researched American polarization have also ruminated on its cultural impact. Shanto Iyengar and Sean J. Westwood demonstrate how the increasing vitriol and open expression of hatred between Left and Right on a popular level (partisans) that we've chronicled in this chapter is a disincentive for cooperation among our government officials (elites). On an elite level, this cycle leads to a government paralyzed by its polarization. The Republican Tea Party that began during Barack Obama's presidency gave way to a Democratic "Resistance" during Donald Trump's time in office. With little incentive to collaborate, legislators hurl opposition across the aisle, and not much governing is accomplished.

This influence also runs in the opposite direction. "If anything," Iyengar and Westwood write, "the rhetoric and actions of political leaders demonstrate that hostility directed at the opposition is acceptable, even appropriate."[21] So it's come to this: as the venerable chambers of the US Congress look every day more like a middle-school lunchroom, the people Congress governs follow suit. The people's crass partisan resistance then, in turn, emboldens leaders to refuse to cooperate in ways that license the people to increase their mutual disdain for one another, and so on. Caught in the vicious cycle, relationships across difference spiral downward into increasingly heated confrontation and opposition. It's no wonder that one in ten divorces in the months after the 2016 election stemmed from how each member of the couple had voted.[22]

A CHILLING SYMBOL

In the early morning of June 14, 2017, as Republican congresspersons practiced baseball on a field in Alexandria, Virginia, a gunman named James Hodgkinson saw his opportunity. He made his way to the practice field, inquired to confirm the identity of his targets, and opened fire. His shotgun scatter-shooting struck four of the representatives before nearby Capitol Police agents shot and killed him. He hit Steve Scalise, the majority whip and a representative from Louisiana, in the hip, so that Scalise remained in critical condition for months afterward.

The shooter hailed from the apocalyptically frustrated Left. He could see no way forward with "them," so he planned his route, parked his van, and began pulling the trigger. As I read the news, my mind wandered back to Charleston in 2015, when an apocalyptically frustrated alt-right young man named Dylann Roof opened fire on a Wednesday-evening Bible study to get rid of another "them." In a symbolic sense, this shooter was an extreme version of all of us. When Barack Obama took power, a host of right-wingers mounted his picture on their target and went to war because he and his political kind were the problem. And after Donald Trump's victory in November 2016, normally nonviolent progressives even contemplated Dietrich Bonhoeffer's solution to Hitler: assassinate the problem.

The Hodgkinson story is a parable for the United States in our time. We are a nation of white supremacists, Left supremacists, and Right supremacists. We live by a violent credo: If you can't beat them, shoot them (Alexandria and Charlston). Or if you can't shoot them, run over them (Charlottesville) or shout them down (Claremont McKenna College) or rough them up (Middlebury College) or cancel their speeches (UC Berkeley) or walk out on them (the University of Notre Dame) or agitate to fire them or threaten to kill them (Evergreen State College) or deny them their right to vote or just block their views and news.[23] We live with the stunted, simplistic, utterly immature conviction that the world will only ever be better without "them."

On that fateful June Wednesday morning, James Hodgkinson's dreaded "they," the Republicans, were practicing baseball. Congressman Scalise and others were stretching little-used muscles, dusting off neglected shoes and gloves, and preparing to embarrass themselves a little less than they might have when they walked on Nationals Field for Thursday night's annual Red-versus-Blue charity game. Another "they," the team of Democrats, were surely practicing elsewhere for the same reason. Game time was a day away.

That's the funny thing about baseball, though. Without "them," there's no game. Without "them," we don't practice, improve, or enjoy. Without "them," we're left standing stupidly, purposelessly, on the field alone. Just as it seems that our self-destructive rock bottom has been reached, our fantasies and realities grow even more violent. In our current American dreams, we are actually fantasizing a political killer's pure-type: life without "them."

SEEKING A SOLUTION

The nation needs leaders who see that the road we're walking leads to mutual destruction and who offer us a path back toward one another. In theory, the movement that Jesus imagined and began to build would seem perfect for the purpose. After all, Jesus challenged his disciples with one "new commandment" for them: "Love one another as I have loved you." And he promised that following this command would have wide impact. If they would love one another, he said, the watching world would know "that you are my disciples" (John 13:34–35). Later in John's Gospel, Jesus prayed, "not only for my disciples but for those who will believe through their words, that they all may be one" (17:20–21). And the impact of this love-forged unity would also radiate beyond the boundary of the group. When the church is "one," Jesus assured them, "the world will believe that you [God] have sent me and that you [God] love them as you loved me" (17:23). The Apostle Paul used the metaphor of a body to picture a community of people who differ from one another but form one functioning organism together, in which there are no "divisions among you" (1 Corinthians 1:11) and "there is neither Jew nor Greek, slave nor free, male and female, but we are all one in Christ Jesus" (Galatians 3:28). And he imagined that all this family unity would make us "shine as lights in the world" (Philippians 2:15). Christian love and unity are designed not merely as a feel-good practice; God intends them to do nothing less than change the society in which Christians reside. At least that's what it looked like on Jesus's whiteboard. Alas, it hasn't worked out that way yet.

Notes

1. Abraham Lincoln, "House Divided Speech," Springfield, IL, June 16, 1858, http://tinyurl.com/ydgqk9pq.

2. Former American diplomats with experience in Rwanda, South Sudan, and "years of observing political transitions" in other countries, as one of them puts it, have been asked to estimate this probability. The estimates range, but average in the 35 percent range. See Keith Mines, "Will We Have Civil War?" in *Foreign Policy* March 10, 2017 (http://tinyurl.com/y7d9l8gt) and especially Thomas Ricks, "Will We Have a 2nd Civil War?" You Tell Me. In *Foreign Policy* March 7, 2017 (http://tinyurl. com/ychvaeqp).

3. James Davison Hunter, *Culture Wars: The Struggle to Define America* (New York: Harper Collins, 1991). The term "Culture War" (*Kulturkampf*) first appears to describe the late nineteenth-century battle for the soul of the German Empire between Chancellor Bismarck's vision for German culture and the Roman Catholic Church. See Martin Spahn, "Kulturkampf," The Catholic Encyclopedia 8 (New York: Robert Appleton, 1910), http://tinyurl.com/y7qogn43.

4. Institute for Advanced Studies in Culture, University of

Virginia, "Survey Finds 'Two Nations in One,'" news release, September 19, 2016, http://tinyurl.com/ybjoxj7n.

5. Robert Gehl, "Here Comes the Evil: The Left Reacts to the Death of Antonin Scalia," The Federalist Papers Project, February 13, 2016, http://tinyurl.com/y8fo6ml7; Nancy French, "Six Prominent Liberals Celebrate Scalia's Death on Twitter," *French Revolution* (blog), February 16, 2016, http://tinyurl.com/yc7meu5d; Kristine Marsh, "Twelve Tweets of Liberal Journalists Celebrating Scalia's Death," MRC NewsBusters blog, February 15, 2016, http://tinyurl.com/y9ykz9rj.

6. Ben Schreckinger, "Trump Rally Speaker Fantasizes about Death of Hillary Clinton," *Politico*, October 30, 2016, http://tinyurl.com/y8c5jwl6.

7. Ta-Nehisi Coates has said that in the antebellum period, the United States was declaring war on its own through slavery. In a defense to critics of that claim, Coates asks important questions about what can properly be called a war. "One notion which I bear little respect for is the idea that the term 'war' should be reserved for countries that can field mass quantities of armed men. I am reminded of the old quote that the difference between a dialect and a language is that the latter enjoys an army. . . . Surely if we can take Al Qaeda's actions as a declaration of war, if we can declare war on 'terror' on 'drugs' on 'illiteracy,' if Gaddafi can be said to have 'made war upon

his people,' then I find little wrong with the claim that a country can declare war upon its own." Ta-Nehisi Coates, "The Midwife of American Freedom," *Atlantic*, May 17, 2012, http://tinyurl.com/ydxoammc.

8. Shanto Iyengar and Sean J. Westwood, "Fear and Loathing across Party Lines: New Evidence on Group Polarization," *American Journal of Political Science* 59, no. 3 (July 2015), 6: http://tinyurl.com/yd84bsfo. Emphasis added.

9. Cass R. Sunstein, "'Partyism' Now Trumps Racism," *Bloomberg View*, September 22, 2014, http://tinyurl.com/ yaylad2e.

10. S. Iyengar and Westwood, "Fear and Loathing across Party Lines." The data are summarized and made accessible by Cass Sunstein in "'Partyism' Now Trumps Racism." In tension with this evidence is a survey by the Pew Research Center that found much lower percentages (15 and 17 percent) when they asked adult respondents, "Would you be upset if someone in your family married a Republican/Democrat?" Drew DeSilver, "How the Most Ideologically Polarized Americans Live Different Lives," *FactTank*, (Pew Research Center blog), June 13, 2014, http://tinyurl.com/ydejeqgy. See also Morris Fiorina, *Culture Wars: The Myth of a Polarized America* (New York: Pearson, 2004).

11. Brian Resnick, "A New Brain Study Sheds Light on Why

It Can Be So Hard to Change Someone's Political Beliefs," *Vox*, January 23, 2017, http://tinyurl.com/y9c6er4v.

12. Jonas T. Kaplan, Sarah I. Gimbel, and Sam Harris, "Neural Correlates of Maintaining One's Political Beliefs in the Face of Counterevidence," *Scientific Reports* 6, article 39,589 (2016), doi:10.1038/srep39589, available at http://tinyurl.com/jfd7yfy.

13. Bill Bishop, *The Big Sort: Why the Clustering of Like-Minded American Is Tearing Us Apart* (New York: Houghton Mifflin, 2009), 15.

14. Bishop, *The Big Sort*, 14. A 2014 Pew Research Center study confirms and updates the evidence for Bishop's thesis. A 2013 piece confirms and updates Bishop's thesis. Wendy K. Tam Cho, James G. Gimpel, and Iris S. Hui, "Voter Migration and the Geographic Sorting of the American Electorate," *Annals of the Association of American Geographers* 103, no. 4 (2013): http://tinyurl.com/yc4ewme5.

15. Emily Badger et al., "This Election Highlighted a Growing Rural-Urban Split," *New York Times*, November 11, 2016, http://tinyurl.com/yd3fjjmc.

16. Michael Tesler, "Trump Voters Think African Americans Are Much Less Deserving than 'Average Americans,'" *Huffington Post*, December 19, 2016, http://tinyurl.com/y73h78dg.

17. Charles M. Blow, "Trump's Rural White America," *New York Times*, November 14, 2016, http://tinyurl.com/yd9hdsg7.

18. For a humorous entry point to the cycle, see Loey Nunning, "Six Big Differences That Turn City Dwellers into Liberals," *Cracked*, February 18, 2017, http://tinyurl.com/ybtyqal5.

19. David Usborne, "North Carolina Transgender Bathroom Law Prompts Boycotts as Anger Grows," *Independent*, May 1, 2016, http://tinyurl.com/ybtkc23q; Fr. Mark Hodges, "NBA and NFL Turn Up Heat on North Carolina over Transgender Bathrooms," *LifeSite*, June 6, 2016, http://tinyurl.com/y7md495b.

20. "Tow Truck Driver Leaves Woman Stranded after Seeing Bernie Sanders Sticker," WGN (Chicago), May 5, 2016, http://tinyurl.com/hl9rfzz.

21. Iyengar and Westwood, "Fear and Loathing across Party Lines."

22. These break-ups have been given the name, "Trump Divorces." See the anecdotes and statistics in Megan Carullo's *NY Daily News* piece, "Trump Presidency Is Destroying Marriages across the Country," August 5, 2017, http://tinyurl.com/yakvv9wq.

23. For Charlottesville, see "Car Rams Charlottesville Crowd after Protests," *USA Today*, August 13, 2017,

https://tinyurl.com/ycybe9j5; for Claremont McKenna College, "Protestors Disrupt Talk by Pro-Police Author, Sparking Free-Speech Debate at Claremont McKenna College" Howard Blume, *LA Times*, April 9, 2017, https://tinyurl.com/y79cdvr4; for Middlebury College, Peter Beinart, "A Violent Attack on Free Speech at Middlebury College," *The Atlantic*, March 6, 2017, https://tinyurl.com/zhek3zl; Liam Stack, "Notre Dame Students Walk Out of Mike Pence Commencement Address," *New York Times*, May 21, 2017, https://tinyurl.com/ybt5evnm; for Evergreen State, Joe Sterling, "Classes at Washington College Canceled Again amid Threats," June 5, 2017, CNN.com, https://tinyurl.com/y856uaok; on voting rights, Anna North, "Five Ways Republicans Are Threatening Voting Rights," *New York Times*, Nov 7, 2016, https://tinyurl.com/ybxlf2wm.

2

A TALE OF TWO PRAYERS

Whatever disunites people from God also disunites people from people.

—Edmund Burke

In August 1986, I arrived on the Princeton Theological Seminary campus to begin work toward a master's of divinity, feeling both excited and wary. My world was getting bigger. I had lived till then in the villages and towns of western Oregon. "Century Farms"—acreage that has been in the family for a whole century—were a big deal. When I got off the train in Princeton, nearly four centuries of American and church history surrounded me. Old buildings, old families, and old churches would become normal to me, and I'd have friends and classmates from just about everywhere.

Amid all this cultural and historical bliss, I did carry a small measure of theological wariness. I'd been warned, you see. Two months before I traveled to Princeton, the elders of my little country Evangelical Quaker church in Newberg, Oregon, walked me down to the meeting house basement one weekday, wearing faces lined with grave sobriety. These were the kindest and best of men. They had ushered me through my college years with wise counsel and a ready eye watching for ways to help me mature as a disciple of Jesus. Now, though, they were clearly concerned. As they sat me down amid their circle of folding chairs, these spiritual leaders prayed passionately that God would keep me safe and secure my salvation as I traveled to the liberal east.

Fast-forward a decade and a half, to New Haven, Connecticut, at the beginning of fall semester at Yale Divinity School, where I heard another passionate prayer. I was now on faculty at one of those east-coast schools my prayer warriors had so feared. That afternoon, we chatted, as professors do, about students and committee work and the summer research we'd finished (or not finished). These were excellent men and women—brilliant scholars and supportive mentors to me as I learned the ropes of academe. Our conversation that day eventually found its way to the admissions process and expectations about the incoming class. In a moment of unplugged honesty, one long-time holder-forth let out a long sigh and said, "Lord, I can deal with low IQs and bad writing style. But please, in your mercy, let there be no Evangelicals!"

Both of these prayers live uneasily in my memory. They were both uttered by good people, my mentors and exemplars, who nonetheless nursed a sort of bigotry. Both my evangelical Quaker elders and my faculty colleagues saw their theological opposites as, at best annoying, and at worst dangerous. These pray-ers surely would not have confessed to hating people on the other end of the Christian continuum, but from where I stood, they looked on the other with a mix of fear and righteous disdain. I know that everyone in this picture was trying to get Christianity right, but both sides had somehow arrived at the self-serving conclusion that they themselves had succeeded in that effort while their opposite number had failed miserably.

These two episodes had another characteristic in common: they both occurred before political polarization would ramp up in years hence. Our American Christian division and other-loathing has climbed far enough fast enough in the two intervening decades to make these two little prayers feel a little quaint in comparison.

CHRISTIAN COMPLICITY

We Christians have either caught or caused America's bad habit—probably a bit of both. If our nation weren't at war with itself, the vehemence of our Christian disagreements might be less damning. Theological anger can, after all, lead to better church and better work in the world. But the fires of polarization do blaze, making our squabbles worse than luxury. And this conflagration isn't any one issue from the culture wars list. The fire these days is the fighting itself. That's what stops government in its tracks, threatens basic civility in neighborhoods and in classrooms, blows up our campuses at commencement speech time, and gives us enemies in our own towns. And here's the scary truth: we aren't just ignoring the fire or blaming others for it; we're throwing gas on it.

As we judge one another, neither Christian side seeks a truce or reconciliation that could lead to collaboration and shared community. And we ought to note how readily we use the language of two sides about the church. Instead of coming together, as Jesus commanded in John 13:34–35 and prayed

17:20–23, left- and right-wing Christians mostly array ourselves on one side of the chasm or the other and push to widen it. In a nation that is still three quarters Christian, right now, we're the problem.

THE ISSUE WITH OUR GENES

We twenty-first-century Christians come by our divisiveness honestly: we have inherited it from our ancient Christian ancestors. In spite of Jesus's prayer "that they all may be one," our first-century founders sometimes acted more like enemies than friends. The earliest churches battled one another over everything from how to distribute the offering plate money (Acts 6), to which of their prophets spoke truth and which falsehood (Matthew 7; Revelation 2–3; Didache 10), to whether Moses's law provided access to God or threw up a blockade on the pathway to God (Matthew 5; Galatians 1–4; James 2–3). In fact, the same Johannine community that gave us the Gospel with Jesus's prayer for Christian unity (John 17:20–23), also gave us one of the most striking versions of early Christian division (2 John 10–11).

These disagreements alone do not convict our ancient forebears. Robust debate ought to be a part of any community that cares for ideas. But their differences sometimes produced strife. They called one another dogs and evildoers and whores (Philippians 3:1; Revelation 2:20), wished one another bodily harm (Galatians 5:12), called curses down on one another (Galatians 1:8–9), and refused to eat together or share living space (2 John 10–11). Even given ancient standards of polemic,[1] these words are harsh, but it's difficult to detect from scripture how often that conflict led them to disown one another altogether. We don't know whether Paul and the author of James ever worshiped together or excommunicated one another.

As the fledgling church grew and organized itself into a network headed by bishops, those first-century theological battles between itinerant leaders began to bear the weight of "the church." Christians began to define an orthodoxy and track the perilous violators. A century after the apostle Paul's ministry, a Roman Christian called Marcion, who loved Paul's writings, found nothing good at all in the Hebrew Scriptures or its God. The New Testament as we know it hadn't been established yet in 150 CE, so Christians used the books that helped them most. Communities in different cities read and used different books. Among the books available to him, Marcion chose his own "canon"—one of the first we know. He chose Paul's letters and parts of Luke's Gospel, and by his dissent from some definitions of orthodoxy in his day, Marcion earned the title (on some lists) of first official heretic.[2]

During this same stretch of second-century time, some Christians gravitated to the intellectual and mystical parts of Jesus's teaching much more than the material and behavioral parts. Although the movement took various forms, these "Gnostics" practiced a Christianity that focused on the spiritual, intellectual, and esoteric elements of truth. In time, other early Christians, like Bishop Irenaeus of Lugdunum (later Lyon), claimed the authority to officially condemned their writings, so the so-called Gnostics too became "heretics."

A certain Montanus posed another second-century challenge to the prevailing orthodoxy. In his little town of Pepuza, in present-day Turkey, this charismatic leader claimed that God's Holy Spirit had directly inspired his words. Rumor had it that, before his conversion to Christianity, Montanus had been a priest of Apollo or Cybele, with the power to prophesy directly from the god. His energy attracted followers who honored his status as God's spokesman and believed in spiritual revelations. He and his group also drew the ire of the orthodox hierarchy, who declared them heretics.

This process of defining the theological outsiders escalated after Constantine, when Christian leaders could call on the arms and political power of Rome to enforce an orthodoxy. From the fourth century through the beginning of the sixteenth, the Roman Church ruled Christianity in the West, and that sometimes meant forcibly putting down difference and dissent, whether through inquisitions or heresy trials or the simple threat of excommunication. This orientation to theological and religious difference produced the infamous Inquisitions of the thirteenth through seventeenth centuries. Over the last two of those centuries, in a post-Reformation world, scholars estimate that the organs of the Spanish Inquisition alone account for three thousand to five thousand executions, all to exterminate doctrinal heresy.[3]

A half millennium ago, in the autumn of 1517, the Wittenberg monk Martin Luther hammered ninety-five theses on the Castle Church door, hoping to start a conversation. Within three years, the pope excommunicated Luther. But unlike the Marcionites, Montanists, Gnostics, and other "heretics" whose movements are now known mostly to church historians, Luther and his supporters did not quietly fade into oblivion. Armed with the brand-new printing press (Gutenberg minted the first one in 1440) and grateful for a political perfect storm in Europe, Luther had the protection of patrons required for him to stay alive and popularity enough for him to form an alternative network of churches—an amazing accomplishment, given that the Roman Catholic Church had brooked no competition for over a millennium.

The end of exclusive Roman Catholic reign broke open the floodgates. In no time at all, others dissented from Luther's theological claims, and then others dissented from them, and so on, and so on. And these groups didn't get along with one another. Dissent ultimately led again to physical violence—both between Protestants and Catholics, and between varieties of Protestants. Religious wars plagued Europe from the mid-sixteenth through the seventeenth century. The Thirty Years War began when three angry Protestants threw three representatives of the Holy Roman Empire out of the castle tower in Prague. By its end, the conflict had expanded to include most of Europe, and that war alone claimed 30 percent of the German population.[4]

The Protestant instinct to cut and run in the face of disagreement became chic in the 1500s, and it hasn't lost its popularity even now. At the dawn of this century, the *World Christian Encyclopedia* identified over thirty-three thousand distinct Christian denominations, and the number keeps turning over like a telethon tote board.[5] Are you a Presbyterian? You may choose from twenty-nine different varieties in the United States, including one (the Evangelical Covenant Order of Presbyterians) minted as recently as 2012. Baptist? Sixty-two assortments await you. You Methodists, Episcopalians, Lutherans, Congregationalists, and other "mother ship" denominations have your own large stable of off-shoots. Each of those splinters has a story of difference at its origin.

In the colonies, Puritans burned witches, and dissenters such as John Williams and Anne Hutchinson were exiled or executed. Difference meant tension and, often, violence. American Christians of the eighteenth and nineteenth centuries disagreed about slavery, about the legitimacy of revivals, about the place of Catholicism in American culture.[6] By the late 1800s, Christians also fought one another over the fundamentals of Christian faith, their relationship to science, and the legitimacy of the social gospel. In the early 1900s, conflicts channeled American Christians into two parties through the so-called Fundamentalist-Liberal Controversy.

The Fundamentalist-Liberal Controversy

Legend has it that my dorm room at the aforementioned Princeton Theological Seminary (Alexander Hall, Room 409) had eight decades earlier hosted the formidable Christian fundamentalist J. Gresham Machen. As I arrived to begin my studies, Machen's ghost lived on. During my first days, what seemed to me like a dorm full of young theologians greeted me, wearing "Source Busters" T-shirts. These were the days when Bill Murray, Dan Akroyd, and company wore special suits, carried special guns, and busted through doors to the chorus, "Who ya gonna call?! Ghost Busters!!!" My new dorm mates borrowed that buzz to proclaim their opposition to the hegemony of historical criticism—a way of reading the Bible that begins with the academic questions of the scientist and historian, rather than the spiritual assumption that God inspired it.

My friends called themselves "Source Busters" because they disagreed with the interpretive methods their Introduction to the Old Testament professors were teaching them. One branch of the historical-critical approach scours scripture to distinguish the ancient sources that constitute it. Old Testament scholars had detected four main strands in the first books of the Bible: one (called J) used Yahweh/Jehovah as God's name; a second (E) called God "Elohim"; a third (D) brings the theology of the book of Deuteronomy; and a fourth (P) is primarily concerned with priestly matters. Consequently, my friends' shirts featured "JEDP" in bold black letters, stamped out by the international sign of prohibition: ∅.

The "Source Busters" movement unwittingly (and with tongue in cheek) channeled the spirit of our Alexander Hall forebear, J. Gresham Machen. He had come of age at a time when faithful people grappled over the scientific theories of Charles Darwin and forms of historical criticism that they saw undermining biblical faith.[7] For many Christians, the late 1800s was a period of sorting and responding to the Enlightenment and scientific revolution. They asked honest questions about what to do with miracles in a Newtonian world, what to do with creation in a Darwinian world, and more generally, how to relate the Bible to historical and scientific discoveries and theories that seemed to challenge its claims.

As you might expect, Christians reacted variously to modernism.[8] In the midst of all this sorting, a prominent pastor and evangelist named R. A. Torrey planted his flag in 1909 by coediting the influential twelve-volume series *The Fundamentals: A Testi-*

mony to the Truth.[9] In it, Torrey and others named the nonnegotiable beliefs of "true Christians":

1. The Inspiration and Inerrancy of Scripture
2. The Deity of Jesus Christ
3. The Virgin Birth of Christ
4. The Substitutionary Atoning Work of Christ on the Cross
5. The Physical Resurrection and Personal Bodily Return of Christ

Torrey had drawn a line around non-negotiables, and these Fundamentals came to define the boundary lines between two Christianities, which soon became battle lines.

By then a professor at Princeton Seminary, Machen, whose timeless introduction to New Testament Greek has kept him current to generations of theology students, joined Torrey's cause. During his time at Princeton, Machen became increasingly uncomfortable with the modernist theology surrounding him in the seminary and beyond, so he led a conservative revolution among the faculty. He issued his own Declaration of Independence in 1923, with the publication of his boldly titled book *Christianity and Liberalism.*[10] His were fighting words: "In the sphere of religion, in particular, the present time is a time of conflict; the great redemptive religion which has always been known as Christianity is battling against a totally diverse type of religious belief, which is only the more destructive of the Christian faith because it makes use of traditional Christian terminology. This modern non-redemptive religion is called 'modernism' or 'liberalism.'"[11] Even the title of Machen's book—*Christianity and Liberalism*—made it clear that his Venn diagram plots Christianity and liberalism as two non-overlapping circles.

From the other side of the battle line came Harry Emerson Fosdick, fists up. Fosdick volleyed his brand of progressive Christianity from three different Manhattan pulpits over four decades. His sermons opposed fundamentalism wherever he encountered it. Fosdick attended Union Theological Seminary in Manhattan, where he absorbed the modernist theology that pervades his preaching. If Machen felt persecuted by the Left, Fosdick felt besieged by the Right. His sermons led to an investigation of his theology that ultimately would have led to a censure from the national Presbyterian denomination if he hadn't fled to Park Avenue Baptist in 1924 and then to the newly formed Riverside Church.

Fosdick preached his most famous sermon, "Shall the Fundamentalists Win?" from the Park Avenue pulpit in 1922. In that historic message, he targeted a kind of Christian conservative who would "drive out of the evangelical churches men and women of liberal opinions."[12] He bemoaned the antiscientific bent of his denomination's conservative wing and their insistence that any true Christian must believe the Fundamentals. Fosdick opposed this requirement on the grounds that any thinking person of faith must adjust to life and the cosmos as the scientific revolution describes them.

Fosdick ended his forceful attack on fundamentalism with an unintentional but telling mirror image of Machen's exclusionary approach. See if you can spot it: "The Fundamentalists propose to drive out from the Christian churches all the consecrated souls who do not agree with their theory of inspiration. What immeasurable folly! Well, they are not going to do it; certainly not in this vicinity. I do not even know in this congregation whether anybody has been tempted to be a Fundamentalist. Never in this church have I caught one accent of intolerance. God keep us always so!"[13] Did you catch the irony? Fosdick rails against fundamentalist exclusiveness, which "would drive out . . . all . . . who do not agree with their theory of inspiration." Such intolerance will not be tolerated! Then the purportedly inclusive pastor rejoices and congratulates himself because

41

there are none of those intolerant, exclusive sorts in his church. Evidently, he has excluded them

Years later, in his autobiography, Fosdick claimed that the sermon "was a plea for tolerance, for a church inclusive enough to take in both liberals and conservatives without either trying to drive the other out." If so, he missed the mark badly. There's little chance that the fundamentalist in pew 23 could possibly have heard "Shall the Fundamentalists Win?" as an invitation to return the next week. Picture the sermon's Venn diagram. Harry Emerson Fosdick's next book could properly have been titled *Christianity and Fundamentalism*.[14]

Fundamentalists and liberals battled their way through the twentieth century and then into ours. In their mutual excommunications—their refusal to see any overlap between the set "Christian" and the set "those other guys"—Machen and Fosdick embody the hostile failure to love across difference against which Jesus prayed and Paul wrote. The church of the twentieth and twenty-first centuries would follow their lead and extend their battle beyond theological issues to social and political ones.

BELL AND HELL

The enmity continues. The Machen-Fosdick battle over doctrine continued to gather force as the twentieth century gave way to the twenty-first. A very public recent measure of the electrical charge at the Left-Right border is the story of Rob Bell. For the first decade of the new century, Evangelicals loved his books and creative NOOMA videos, which became a mainstay in youth and young adult ministries across the land. Then, in 2011, Bell made national news with his controversial book *Love Wins*.

During the first decade of the twenty-first century, Bell's Mars Hill Bible Church in Grand Rapids, Michigan, had grown from a living-room-sized gathering to attendance over ten thousand in its first six years, and his published works widened his influence. But leading a megachurch and gaining a national following didn't put Rob Bell on the cover of *Time* magazine. (One study recently identified twelve hundred megachurches nationwide.[15]) Bell stood out because he very publicly explored and pushed the boundaries of Evangelical Christian beliefs, when he challenged its doctrine of hell and damnation. In *Love Wins: A Book about Heaven, Hell, and the Fate of Every Person Who Ever Lived*, he asked whether the traditional Evangelical belief about hell had biblical roots sufficient to support its central place in the Evangelical message about salvation.

Time magazine took notice when Bell on hell lit a faith firestorm.[16] "Farewell, Rob Bell," tweeted John Piper, the widely influential lead pastor of Bethlehem Baptist Church in Minneapolis—before he had read the book. Justin Taylor, the lead editor for an influential conservative website called *Crossways*, wrote a scathing blog condemning Bell for "deceiving the people with false doctrines" and "moving farther and farther away from anything resembling biblical Christianity." When he wrote this, Taylor had not read *Love Wins* either.

Debris from this explosion landed near my home church in Minnesota. Wayzata Community Church welcomed Rob Bell to speak in our sanctuary as a part of his book tour, soon after the publication of *Love Wins*. Wayzata Church intentionally cultivates a big-tent congregation, hoping to host a variety of theological and political voices, so we were excited to host this one. When I tried to buy ad time on the local Christian radio station, though, I received a rejection email. They didn't want our money.

The station's e-note supplied their reason: "We cannot be associated with a church that so closely associates itself with Rob Bell." This seemed odd to me, in light of the way the New Testament book of

Acts commends a church in Berea that "welcomed [the Apostle Paul's] message very eagerly and examined the scriptures every day to see whether these things were so" (Acts 17:11). I wrote back, suggesting that a Christian writer who raised questions about how true a teaching was to scripture and a congregation that gathered to weigh the truth of his or her argument, Bibles in hand, sounded veritably Berean to me (Acts 17:10–11).[17] The next day, the station's program manager called to explain. He told me that he would have loved to run the ads, but the station faced pressure from the Right, with board members and the president under fire. Their funding hung in the balance.

I later discovered that area Christian bookstores refused even to stock *Love Wins*. Our people had to search out secular booksellers like Barnes and Noble or Amazon to buy it. The battle over Bell even got physical. The shower of excommunications from Piper and Taylor, along with similar outbursts from many other prominent conservative Christian leaders, lit a fire under their tribes. In the year after *Love Wins* was published, Bell received multiple death threats from the enraged faithful and had to begin traveling with a bodyguard.[18]

Let's tally the results. A prominent Christian leader publishes a book that asks faithful, searching questions about God and salvation and makes the *New York Times* bestseller list. But Christian radio stations won't publicize the book tour, Christian bookstores won't put it on their shelves, other church leaders unofficially excommunicate the author, and other Christians threaten the author's life. Military people call this sort of behavior "friendly fire"—shots that land on members of one's own army, "misidentifying the target as hostile."[19] Christians shoot down Christians, perhaps because we interpret disagreement as hostility. As we have seen, though, the marksmen don't think their targets are Christians, so it gets easier to shoot. Somewhere, Salman Rushdie is having a bitter laugh.[20]

CHRISTIANS IN THE CULTURE WARS

The late twentieth-century church moved its battle boundary beyond doctrine. Fundamentalism and evangelicalism had spent the middle years of the century primarily drawing attention for their evangelistic outreach (e.g., by Billy Graham) and doctrinal distinctions. In the eighties, however, Jerry Falwell and the conservative Moral Majority, Pat Robertson and the 700 Club, and James Dobson's Focus on the Family began to pronounce and lobby on social issues like abortion, prayer in schools, and then later homosexuality. They gained political power in the Reagan years and became a fixture.

The most consistently progressive of the mainline Christian denominations in the United States, the United Church of Christ, caught a rare bit of national attention when NBC, CBS, and ABC television networks said no to them. The denomination had labored for decades unnoticed in the vineyard of social justice, proud to have been the first denomination to ordain an African American, a woman, and an openly gay person. They were a church of first inclusions, hoping for a wider audience to appreciate that fact.[21] To remedy their obscurity, during the presidential election season of 2004, the denomination launched their "God Is Still Speaking" campaign, for which they produced television ads juxtaposing their own inclusive ways with the exclusive ways of more conservative churches.

In one of the ads, muscular bouncers in black shirts stand menacingly at the doors of a big-box church, refusing people of color, gays and lesbians, and the disabled. In another, a congregation sits in conservative-church pews, but soon the same kind of "others" are ejected from their seats. The clever campaign grabbed national attention—more so after the networks, which found the ads too controversial, banned them. In the context of a Bush administration proposal for a federal marriage amendment, CBS did not want to be "on one side of a controversial issue."[22] The UCC fired back that during the campaign, the networks had run much more scathing ads "on one side or the other" of "controversial issue[s]."

The conservative Christians in the crosshairs of the ads offered their own public retort. The words of Rev. Dr. R. Albert Mohler, the president of Southern Baptist Theological Seminary, illustrate: "God may still be speaking," Mohler wrote, but "not . . . in the form of a denial of biblical truth and the authentic Gospel." He continued, "The greatest tragedy with regard to this advertising campaign is not the controversy over the ads, but the message the church is trying to communicate in the first place. Christ saves sinners. That is the great good news of the Gospel—for homosexuals and for everyone else."[23] It turns out that the crux of the conflict was still biblical authority, as it had been with Machen and Fosdick. But this time the issues were cultural and political rather than strictly doctrinal.

Let's take stock once again. A progressive community of Christians slammed a conservative one—their own brothers and sisters in Christ— right in front of God and a media-hungry everyone. Then the conservative brothers and sisters slammed them back, also very publicly. So we have Christians punching Christians in public. The apostle Paul, who didn't even want Christians to sue one another in Roman courts (1 Corinthians 6:1–11), would have spun in his grave.

In our time, Christians have stepped into the Left-Right battles over abortion, the Christian identity of the United States, the (im)morality of the entertainment media, gun laws, recreational drug use, immigration, and a host of other issues. Right-wing and left-wing Christian leaders pronounce on these issues and then lather up their like-thinking congregants until they self-righteously dismiss their Christian brothers and sisters on the other side of the issue. Intolerance abounds in both camps.

BACK TO THOSE PRAYERS

Christians are called by Jesus to be one. While we may differ in how we imagine "being one," we can surely agree that it does not look like the self-righteous mutual excommunication we saw in the Inquisitions, the Reformation, and the Machen-Fosdick battle. Nor does "being one" look like the angry political opposition that has produced bouncer commercials from the Left or death threats against Rob Bell from the Right, or any of the other vehement and even violent opposition across Christianity in our time.

We American Christians are kindling the fire of division in our land. As our nation divides down the middle and our government stalls and our communities split and political partisans dance on the graves of the opposition, the church has widened the chasm and joined the stall, the split, and the dance. But by doing this, we thumb our noses at Jesus's claim that our central identifying witness to the world is love for one another (John 13:34–35; 17:20–21). We choose orthodoxy over community, and the cost to both church and republic is great.

THE BLAME GAME

My progressive Christian friends trace this intolerance to judgmental, exclusive fundamentalists. To some extent, they're right. Conservative Christianity has wreaked this havoc. Certainly, the religious Right has played a more public and recognizable role in the culture wars. The Jerry Falwells and Franklin Grahams among us routinely treat Left-Right differences as battle lines, and they carry the power of a considerable public with them. Their mingling of Christian rhetoric with conservative politics leaves many with a strong sense that if we could trace to primary motivations, their Republican identity over-whelms the Christian part.

The blame isn't all theirs, though. Having observed close up the animosity progressive Chris-tians vent toward their conservative counterparts on Facebook posts, tweets, blogs, and pub conversa-tions across these polarized years, I can attest that the vitriol and dehumanizing rhetoric runs both ways and in similar measure. In his May 2016 op-ed piece, "Confessions of Liberal Intolerance," Nico-las Kristof paved the way for a left-wing humility that largely remains the road not taken. He depicts campuses where the vast progressive majority treat conservatives like alien inferiors.[24] Our progressive church leaders often follow suit, oblivious to the notion that the stray conservatives in their midst might be a gift rather than a nuisance.

My point in this book is not to assign blame or adjudicate a better or worse. My goal is to inculcate in all of us a readiness to see that we don't have all the answers and to open ourselves to the prospect that people we've routinely dismissed may have some of them. When I speak with conservative friends, they blame liberals, and liberal friends blame conservatives. When they do this, I feel like I'm back in middle school, hearing the classic, "Well, he started it!" argument. Jesus said, "Let the one who is without sin cast the first stone." I wonder what that caution means in our theological context.

I believe the start of the solution to all that ails us is simple Christian humility. Lillian Daniel has put her finger on a bad habit shared by Left and Right. She recognizes it in her progressive tribe, but it runs both ways. Daniel relays how, in an act of feigned humility that veils condemnation of conser-vatives, progressive preachers apologize for churches that aren't theirs. "An easy apology for me," she writes, "would be 'As a pastor, I apologize for other churches that would not do your gay wedding.'" In this practice, smugness abounds. As Daniel recog-nizes, "Apologizing to strangers for the Salem witch trials is easy when you didn't actually burn any witches. There's no humility in that, especially when you're doing it to make yourself look better in com-parison! Confession is admitting something you actually did and may be still doing."[25]

Conservative pastors play out their own version of this when they thunder from their pulpits with judgment upon "secularized Christians" who don't treat the Bible as God's literal word, compromise the Christian identity of the United States, and so on. Like their progressive counterparts, these "prophets" point their accusing finger at people who are not in the room, not in their tribe. As Daniel points out, this is miles away from honest, humble self-evaluation. It lathers up the gathered faithful by confirming "our" superiority to "them."

I tell you a mystery: even as we all parade our smug superiority and blame the other side, almost everyone in this embattled Christian picture is trying to get it right. It has become normal in our time to assign bad motives to wrong beliefs (as we define them). But that is not my experience at all. In the course of my life, I've drunk deeply of God's Spirit in churches across the whole range of Christian beliefs and practices, from Far Right to Far Left, and I have close friends who span the entire theological spectrum. I can attest that not one of these churches or Christians set out to mess up Christianity or get Jesus wrong.

My Quaker elders and Yale colleagues were trying to get it right, too. And they were some of the best people I've ever known. Yet they couldn't imagine that a liberal Christian seminary, on the one hand, or an Evangelical Christian student, on the other, might contribute something redemptive to their world. If these good and faithful folks couldn't muster that sort of humility, it must be a terribly hard thing to do.

NOTES

1. Luke T. Johnson, "The New Testament's Anti-Jewish Slander and the Conventions of Ancient Polemic," *Journal of Biblical Literature* 108 (1989): 419–41.

2. Glenn Davis, "Early Christian Authorities: Marcion and the Marcionites," *The Development of the Canon of the New Testament*, last revision July 25, 2008, http://tinyurl.com/y8hlq9ly.

3. Henry Kamen, *The Spanish Inquisition: A Historical Revision* (New Haven: Yale University Press, 1999).

4. C. V. Wedgwood, *The Thirty Years War* (New York: New York Review of Books, 2005).

5. "Denominations," *Christianity Today*, n.d., http://tinyurl.com/yd6hmhq2.

6. To learn about the nativist controversy surrounding Catholicism, see Katie Oxx, *The Nativist Movement in America: Religious Conflict in the 19th Century* (New York: Routledge, 2013).

7. Darwin described his theory in *The Descent of Man, and Selection in Relation to Sex.*

8. James R. Moore supplies the spectrum of responses in his book *The Post-Darwinian Controversies* (Cambridge: Cambridge University Press, 1979).

9. R. A. Torrey, A. C. Dixon, et al., eds., *The Fundamentals: A Testimony to the Truth* (AGES Digital Library, 2009), http://tinyurl.com/y8e69nnk.

10. Six years passed between the appearance of *Christianity and Liberalism* and Machen's exodus from Princeton to found the more orthodox Westminster Theological Seminary in Philadelphia. I picture chilly faculty meetings.

11. J. G. Machen, *Christianity and Liberalism* (New York: Macmillan, 1923), available at http://tinyurl.com/y7zezhq3.

12. Harry Emerson Fosdick, "Shall the Fundamentalists Win?" *Christian Work* 102 (June 10, 1922): 716–22, available at http://tinyurl.com/56twxj.

13. Fosdick, "Shall the Fundamentalists Win?"

14. In fact, at the Presbyterian General Assembly of 1923 in Indianapolis, William Jennings Bryan led fundamentalist Presbyterian pastors of his day to plead for Fosdick's removal. First Presbyterian Church in the City of New York, available at http://tinyurl.com/yasflfdy.

15. The Hartford Seminary group sets the attendance mark at two thousand adults and children per weekend. See Scott Thumma and Warren Bird, "Recent Shifts in America's Largest Protestant Churches: Megachurches

2015 Summary Report," Hartford Institute for Religion Research, 2015, http://tinyurl.com/yc5o5kmf.

16. John Meacham, "Pastor Rob Bell: What if Hell Doesn't Exist?," *Time*, April 14, 2011, http://tinyurl.com/y9flu2qw.

17. In Acts 17, Paul praises the Bereans for assiduously fact-checking his message using scripture. That episode has given rise to many Evangelical Bible study groups called "The Bereans." Unfortunately, I've not yet discovered a single progressive-church study group of that name. More on the biblical illiteracy of the Left later.

18. Rev. Dr. John Ross (Senior Minister of Wayzata Community Church) and I heard about the death threats from Rob Bell and his bodyguard during a brief interview at Wayzata Community Church in 2012.

19. Boris Ilchenko, "Friendly Fire in the North Pacific," *North Pacific Skies: People and Machines*, available at http://tinyurl.com/y76rry7s.

20. When Salman Rushdie published his controversial *Satanic Verses* in 1989, the Ayatollah Khomeini launched a persecution that resulted in death threats that forced Rushdie into hiding. At the time, American conservatives and liberals both condemned the intolerance of fundamentalist Muslims. "Looking Back at Salman Rushdie's *Satanic Verses*," *Guardian*, September 14, 2012, http://tinyurl.com/yaxzwmto.

21. United Church of Christ website, UCC Firsts, http://tinyurl.com/yb9on4ze.

22. "Networks Reject Church Gay Ad," *CNN World*, December 1, 2004, http://tinyurl.com/ya57scho.

23. R. Albert Mohler Jr., "Bouncers at the Church Door? A Controversy over Church Ads," AlbertMohler.com, December 3, 2004, http://tinyurl.com/y7f7jg52.

24. Nicholas Kristof, "A Confession of Liberal Intolerance," *New York Times*, May 7, 2016, http://tinyurl.com/zxm73ne.

25. Jonathan Merritt, "This Lent, I'm Giving Up Apologizing for Other Christians," *Religion News*, March 3, 2017, http://tinyurl.com/y8jwdhlp.

3

RIGHTEOUS
MINDS

It is folly to argue against determined hardness;
. . . nothing can reach the heart that is steeled
with prejudice.

—Thomas Paine, *The Crisis*

The Pulitzer Prize–winning novelist Toni Morrison
began research for her novel *Paradise* by coursing
through the many epic imaginings of a blissful after-
life that span literary and religious history. She
searched the epics of Homer and Virgil, Dante and
Milton, along with the biblical book of Revelation
and every other classic depiction she could get her
hands on. Morrison shared her research journey in
a captivating 1995 lecture to a gathering of American
religious scholars in Philadelphia. I was in the audi-

ence that night and I remember her words vividly: "These visions of paradise differ wildly from one another, but three salient themes appear in every one of them: community, eternity, and exclusion. Each picture of the 'sweet by and by' celebrates the same idyllic vision. She paused for effect. 'That's right, you and me together, forever . . . without them!'"[1]

What Toni Morrison says about paradise, you and I know from experience. Her summary of these visions of paradise describes well an origin of American polarization, but it also makes clear that twenty-first-century Americans don't corner the market on this habit. Exclusion and a we-they vision of bliss persist in human communities across cultures, and literary examples range from the sublime to the ridiculous. Shakespeare's mutually loathing Montague and Capulet families made Romeo and Juliet's love story tragic; our children know this dynamic already from nursery school experience by the time story time introduces them to Dr. Seuss's "Star-Bellied Sneeches," who fancy themselves so superior to the plain-bellied sort. And we laugh when *Monty Python's Life of Brian* features the revolutionary People's Front of Judea, who bitterly despise the almost identical but vastly inferior Judean People's Front. These fictional divides forefront the trivial differences that can distinguish group from group and license condescension. But the outcomes of this habit can be anything but trivial. Indian culture defines untouchables by class, and that definition supports millennia of subjugation. In Rwanda, Hutu tribe members loathe Tutsis, and Tutsis, Hutus, and genocide ensued. Ethnic cleansing proceeds afoot in Myanmar as I write. We humans have a habit of defining and gravitating to "our people," then naturally relegating the "other people" to inferior status.

WE-THEY, US-THEM

In the early 2000s, British sociologist David Kelly and a few colleagues set out to discover whether humans enter the world coded for racial preference. In our race-divided world, these researchers asked whether we emerge from the womb favoring people like us or learn our prejudice along life's way. Theirs is the old nature-or-nurture question revisited.

To answer it, Kelly and his team explored the way newborns and infants recognize and process sense data as they observe faces. They chose representative photographic images of Caucasian, Asian, Middle Eastern, and African faces. Then they cast these images, one by one, on a screen where newborns could see them. To determine the disposition of the pre-speech infants toward the images, they measured how long each child focused on each image and then compared the results. Kelly and his crew discovered that, on their first day outside the womb, these newborns lingered for roughly the same amount of time on faces across the races. They did not prefer the image that reflected their own race. Significantly, in these infants' first experience of their world, any face was as compelling as any other.

The story changed, though, within a mere ninety developmental days. The same team of scientists placed three-month-old infants in precisely the same conditions as they had the newborns, flashed the same array of images, and again measured the length of gaze. This time, though, after three months outside the womb, the infants fixed and lingered longer on the faces that matched their own caregivers' ethnicities. In other words, within three months, the infants had developed a preference, not only for the face of the specific person who most often looked after her or him, but, more importantly, for other faces that resembled that person ethnically—for her or his "people." The study proved that human standard equipment does not include "preferential selectivity based on ethnic differences," but that we develop it very quickly, within the first three months of life, on the basis of familiarity.[2]

The equipment we use to differentiate our tribe continues to develop. If we quickly learn to spot and prefer "our people," we also lose interest in the specifics of "other people." Research has nuanced these findings about preference by demonstrating that a short while after we begin to prefer our own kind (between five and nine months of age), in spite of rapidly improving sense and observation faculties, developing infants become less—rather than more—able to recognize emotional cues in cross-race faces.

As in real estate, so in brain science, location matters. Studies have located these functions within the geography of the brain, showing that between the fifth and the ninth month, the recognition of emotions in or outside races moves from the front of the brain, where the function is attention, to a section near the back of the brain, where we process perceptions.[3] That means our new skills at differentiating "we" from "they" has migrated from the brain's temporary files to its system files. Clearly, as infants experience more and more faces of the same race, they become oriented to that race, recognize fewer details in the faces of other races, and begin to store that disparity deeper in their brain's processing centers.

We're programmed to differentiate our kind from

others early. Infant humans quickly learn to sort people and gravitate to our groups. Born without bias, we are genetically groomed to gather sense information that will help us identify the people like us. We are so adept at it, in fact, that within a quarter year of our lives, we begin to prefer our familiar ethnic in-group and, by three-quarters of a year, to disregard our unfamiliar ethnic out-groups.

FLOCKING TOGETHER

Next, we form groups. The same intellectual equipment that sorts for race also predisposes us to flock together around other forms of sameness as life goes on. In fact, social psychologists tell us that it doesn't take much to arouse that groupish instinct. Trivial and accidental shared traits, like enjoying the same painting or having shirts of the same color, have produced, not only a sense of joint belonging among research subjects, but also a strong preference for in-group members.[4] We celebrate and bond with other sophomores (accidental) or Delta Gammas (elective) or left-handed people (accidental) or United Auto Workers or Evangelicals or progressives or Republicans or Democrats (elective). And we've been this way for a long time. Across cultures and throughout history, this instinct to identify with a group has been endemic to the human species. You may have noticed that over the last half century, prominent sociologists like Robert Bellah (*Habits of the Heart*) and Robert Putnam (*Bowling Alone*) have warned us about the decline of group-joining in American culture. But, to parody Mark Twain's words, reports of the death of groups have been greatly exaggerated. We do groups differently now. My fourteen-year-old son recently met his best friends in the world for the first time, after a year as classmates and chat mates in an online school. Despite the isolating technology that makes us more self-sufficient than ever in human history, we still gravitate to one another.[5]

Human beings naturally seek groups. As you might imagine, sociologists have come up with reasons for this drive. Generally, they say, groups form "when people become dependent on one another for the satisfaction of their needs."[6] We simply feel better in human company; hence our "pervasive drive to form and maintain at least a minimum quantity of lasting, positive, and impactful interpersonal relationships."[7] But the vague claim that "we feel better" in groups than alone hardly satisfies our curiosity. Inquiring minds want to know why.

Researchers identify the rewards and advantages that motivate us to form groups. Some name a basic human need for self-esteem,[8] which naturally increases when a group includes us.[9] (Think of the middle-schooler who gets an invite to the cool-kid table—or at least her idea of what's cool—in the cafeteria.) Additionally, we seek in-groups to help us check the accuracy of or (more often) to bolster our personal beliefs and attitudes.[10] (Think of the protest marchers who report that they show up more to confirm they're not crazy in their dissent than to challenge policy.) When it comes to our core values and convictions, there's strength in numbers, especially under duress or amid ambiguity.[11]

HOW IN-GROUPS EVOLVED

"Why do we like the taste of Skittles and not the taste of shoe leather?" Evolutionary psychologists ask questions like this, that you and I run right past without noticing. Then they work to supply answers that make sense of our ways within a broad Darwinian, survival-of-the-fittest behavioral model. Our long-ago ancestors ate mostly vegetables with occasional "treats" of very tough and very lean meat. In that context, the rare chance at low-hanging fruit offered a dense, quick supply of nutrients. Identifying and pursuing sweet or very fatty foods offered species an obvious advantage. And there's the answer: low-hanging fruit tastes sweeter, and, hundreds of thousands of years later, you and I are tempted to stop at the candy counter, then grab a Coke on our way to Ben and Jerry's.[12]

In this context, human gravitation to groups challenges our usual take on Darwin. Popular perceptions of Charles Darwin's model picture the classic "survival of the fittest" in individual terms: "it's a dog-eat-dog world," after all, and each dog is on her or his own. So, if you and I are trained by hundreds of thousands of years of individualistic survival, why do we like groups so much? That's the question. To answer it, sociobiologists have scoured evolutionary history to locate the specific moment when "feeling better" became the reward for being in groups.

Call it the group advantage. These scientists trace our groupish instincts to a period when species discovered that teams could survive more successfully than lone individuals. Creatures who divided labor—"You watch the food store, and I'll get more!"—outdueled even the most highly adapted individuals for the resources necessary to survival. In nature, species that team up share one common purpose for their cooperation: the defense of a common nest or food source.[13] This makes sense, right? Functioning teams naturally beat even strong individuals in almost every competition we can imagine.

The same logic holds true for human survival. In fact, popular twenty-first-century reality TV shows like *Survivor* and *Big Brother* showcase this strategy through the sophomoric drama of self-interested conspiracies.[14]

"Group selection . . . happens whenever individuals find ways to suppress selfishness and work as a team, in competition with other teams," writes New York University professor Jonathan Haidt, and "human nature is . . . groupish. . . . Our minds contain a variety of mental mechanisms that make us adept at promoting our group's interests, in competition with other groups."[15] One unique part of that equipment is the ability to share intentions. You motion to me to lift the branch, so I do that. You grab the fruit. I tell you to stay and guard the fruit. I forage to find more. We win!

Many thousands of years later, when people learned to share their intentions with much larger groups, they formed social norms for their whole clan.[16] The progression is clear: first, small groups beat individuals, then more cohesive groups bested less cohesive ones, and then large groups (call them tribes) beat small ones, even if they were cohesive. Every time the adaptive innovation prevailed, it reproduced that trait and passed on that habit. Our battle-tested DNA combines with a socialized sense of advantage to tilt us toward groups. Teams and clans have made people healthier and safer, making it a small step from this advantage to an evolutionary sweetener: we feel better in groups.

All of this is splendid to this point—idyllic, even. All humanity sings out the immortal words of Mel Brooks's king in *History of the World, Part One*: "I love my people! My people love me!" As Haidt puts it, "Once you understand our dual nature, including our groupish overlay, you can see why happiness comes from between. We evolved to live in groups."[17]

There is a shadow side, though, to this romantic image of groups. After all, in that scene from *History of the World, Part One*, after proclaiming his enthusiastic love for "[his] people," the king raises his gun and shouts, "Pull!" and a catapult tosses an abject serf across the sky like a clay pigeon. That's because the natural flip side of in-group definition and mutual loyalty is an increased awareness of the boundary between "our people" and "those other people"—say, between aristocrats and serfs—who have their eyes on the same fruit tree I currently guard. We call the two elements of this social dynamic "in-group favoritism" and "out-group derogation."[18] Their bi-play moves us closer and closer to the in-group's sense of superiority, and so to "the righteous mind."

OUR RIGHTEOUS MINDS

Crosby asked me what my name was and what my business was. I told him, and his wife Hazel recognized my name as an Indiana name. She was from Indiana, too.

"My God," she said, "are you a Hoosier?" I admitted I was. "I'm a Hoosier, too," she crowed. "Nobody has to be ashamed of being a Hoosier."

"I'm not," I said. "I never knew anybody who was."

Kurt Vonnegut's novel *Cat's Cradle* illustrates more fully than he intended just how endemic groupishness and an attendant arrogance are. When Hazel and Jonah discover that they both happen to hail from the same 36,418-square-mile patch of arbitrarily bounded land, called Indiana, despite having never met and having little else in common, they suddenly realize that they belong together. Hoosiers are quite a superior-feeling lot in *Cat's Cradle*.

In the vocabulary of *Cat's Cradle*, artificially constructed associations like Hoosiers are called "Gran-falloons," and Vonnegut detests them, judging by his ruthless satire. Granfalloons are shallow associations, mirages of connection. Because, as an existentialist, the author celebrates the individual's lonely quest for meaning, he finds such artificial associations meaningless and even distasteful. His authorial disdain drips from the pages of the novel.

There is a subtle irony here that drives home the hold that our groupishness has on us. Vonnegut seems not to have intended a next layer of group-related meaning that lies beyond the lines of his story. You see, cynical forebears, his literary and philosophical mentors, passed to him this value on the heroic, self-sufficient, meaning-making individual. We call their loosely connected school "existentialists." They wear black turtlenecks and drink similar wines. Ironically, then, the anti-groupish, heroically individualistic Kurt Vonnegut and his like-minded existentialist colleagues ultimately make up a group who count themselves superior to people who need such groups. Existentialists: the anti-group group.

The tendency to rate ourselves and our people as superior to others pervades in human community as much as groupishness does. As Haidt writes, "An obsession with righteousness (leading inevitably to self-righteousness) is the normal human condition. It is a feature of our evolutionary design, not a bug or error that crept into minds that would otherwise be objective and rational."[19] In-group arrogance comes standard-issue with the species.

Given a few minutes and a bit of honest reflection, you'll recognize these tendencies in yourself. On issues ranging from what television shows or sports teams we like to our most cherished theological and political convictions, you and I count ourselves and our co-believers on the side of the angels, and we know where that leaves the people who like that other show or team or just believe that other way. We humans are bred for in-group superiority. It has helped us survive.

I have discovered to my shame the power of this tendency to self-righteousness. I'm writing a book that hopes to undermine a tribal sense of superiority over our ideological other. But as one of the enlightened few who recognize and actively resist that native sense of political or theological superiority over "those Evangelicals" or "those progressives," I'm often tempted to scorn or disdain you oblivious, arrogant people who relish your own tribe. Yes, that's right: I sometimes feel superior about not feeling superior! But wait. Are you feeling superior to me for being that way? It's okay. It comes with the species.

As much sense as all this makes, it only gets us so far in our quest to understand American polarization. We've come full circle and seen how scientists support Toni Morrison's literature-based portrait of human paradise: "You and me together, forever, without them." Tribes, nations, political parties, and all the other identity-anchoring human clusters have felt superior to one another and divided from "the other" in every age and place for around a million years. But we began this book by noticing that American polarization and its particular brand of self-righteous superiority have reached all-time highs in the late twentieth and early twenty-first centuries. Sociologists tell us that our current crop of Americans are more politically polarized than any generation in our history. Conservatives fantasize about a Democrats' deaths and progressive revelers dance on a deceased Supreme Court justice's grave. We're on "righteous mind" steroids. So, granting the innate in-groupishness of all humanity across time, we ought to wonder what makes the righteous mind spike so spectacularly here and now.

NOTES

1. Toni Morrison spoke these words in a plenary address at the annual meeting of the American Academy of Religion and Society of Biblical Literature in Philadelphia in 1995.

2. David J. Kelly, Paul C. Quinn, Alan M. Slater, Kang Lee, Alan Gibson, Michael Smith, Liezhong Ge, and Olivier Pascalis, "Three-Month-Olds, but Not Newborns, Prefer Own-Race Faces," *Developmental Science* 6 (2005): F31–F36.

3. Margaret Vogel, Alexandra Monesson, and Lisa S. Scott, "Building Biases in Infancy: The Influence of Race on Face and Voice Emotion Matching," *Developmental Science* 15 (2012): 359–72. For the distinction between attention and perception, see Pascale Michelon, "What Are Cognitive Abilities and Skills, and How to Boost Them?," *SharpBrains*, December 18, 2006, http://tinyurl.com/yaznz5sy. For a popular presentation of the data, see "Babies Develop Racist Traits Aged Nine Months, before Coming into Contact with Other Races," *Daily Mail*, May 4, 2012, http://tinyurl.com/c5f325s.

4. Henri Tajfel, "Experiments in Intergroup Discrimination," *Scientific American* 223, no. 5 (1970): 96–102. Henri Tajfel, M. G. Billig, R. P. Bundy, and Claude Flament, "Social Categorization and Intergroup

Behaviour," *European Journal of Social Psychology* 2 (1971): 149–78.

5. Kelly's and others' research reveal a universal human desire to find and cluster with people like us. But our twenty-first-century American minds experience some cognitive dissonance here. We've witnessed a quarter century of jeremiads from respected social scientists sound the alarm: Americans are bowling alone. Research by Robert Bellah (*Habits of the Heart* [Berkeley: University of California Press, 1985]), Robert Putnam (*Bowling Alone* [New York: Simon & Schuster, 1995]), and Marc Dunkelman (*The Vanishing Neighbor* [New York: W. W. Norton, 2014]) has led these authors and others to sound the alarm about our "utilitarian individualism," our "social dislocation," and "the disappearance of the neighbor" in American culture. First televisions, then computers, and now social media are named among the culprits in this crime story, because they steal our time together by approximating it virtually. Putnam's analogical indictment is representative of their tone: "TV-based politics is to political action as watching ER is to saving someone in distress."

Bellah, Putnam, Dunkelman, and others have a point. They help us to ask whether we as a culture want to continue on this individualizing trajectory—whether this way leads ultimately to our flourishing. Nonetheless, they overstate the case. The fact is that most people in the United States still gravitate to groups. We are less groupish, but we are group finders nonetheless. Even in these days of digital isolation, between 50 and 80 percent of the American population still regularly seek out the company of in-person groups and group events. And that statistic does not account for the huge increase of online groups or other virtual associations with which we now identify. (Dunkelman himself illustrates how groups can form differently through social media, which enables us to sustain closer contact with our less-connected "outer ring" associates.)

6. Richard L. Morland, "The Formation of Small Groups," *Review of Personality and Social Psychology* 8 (1987): 104.

7. Roy F. Baumeister and Mark Leary, "The Need to Belong: Desire for Interpersonal Attachments as a Fundamental Human Motivation," *Psychological Bulletin* 117, no. 3 (1995): 497.

8. J. Crocker and B. Major, "Social Stigma and Self-Esteem: The Self-Protective Properties of Stigma," *Psychological Review* 96, no. 4 (1989): 608–30.

9. Mark R. Leary and Roy F. Baumeister, "The Nature and Function of Self-Esteem: Sociometer Theory," *Advances in Experimental Social Psychology* 32 (2000): 1–62.

10. Leon Festinger, "A Theory of Social Comparison Processes," *Human Relations* 7, no. 2 (1954): 117–40.

11. Stanley Schachter, *The Psychology of Affiliation* (Stanford: Stanford University Press, 1959).

12. As an accessible entryway to this fascinating field of study, I still recommend Robert Wright's now twenty-year-old book, *The Moral Animal: Why We Are the Way We Are; The New Science of Evolutionary Psychology.*

13. Haidt, *The Righteous Mind*, Kindle locations 6620–21. Groupish species also share two additional traits in common: offspring who require a relatively long period of assistance to survive (compared with other species) and intra-species conflict. Under these conditions, the cream of teamwork rose to the top.

14. This advantage apparently began well before *Homo sapiens* appeared on the scene. Biologists point to beehives and ant colonies as evidence that along the evolutionary way, a few subhuman species discovered the advantages of joining forces with one another. These "ultrasocial" species "live in very large groups that have some internal structure, enabling them to reap the benefits of the division of labor." Jonathan Haidt, *The Righteous Mind: Why Good People Are Divided by Politics and Religion*, Kindle ed. (New York: Random House, 2012), Kindle locations 3561–62.

15. Haidt, *The Righteous Mind* (New York: Pantheon, 2012), 190.

16. M. Tomasello, M. Carpenter, J. Call, T. Behne, and H.

Moll, "Understanding and Sharing Intentions," *Behavioral and Brain Sciences* 28 (2005), 675–735.

17. Haidt, *The Righteous Mind*, Kindle locations 4290–92.

18. Miles Hewstone, Mark Rubin, and Hazel Willis, "Intergroup Bias," in *Annual Review of Psychology*, Feb 2002, 575–604, available at http://tinyurl.com/y8zhxv2r.

19. Haidt, *The Righteous Mind*, Kindle location 89.

4

THE PERILS OF ECHO CHAMBERS

Echo Chamber (NOUN)

1 An enclosed space where sound reverberates.

2 An environment in which a person encounters only beliefs or opinions that coincide with their own, so that their existing views are reinforced and alternative ideas are not considered.

—*Oxford Online Dictionary*[1]

Hank and Heather don't get along. In fact, they detest one another. They used to talk at parties, but just last week Heather "unfriended" Hank on Facebook, because his amped-up screeds against universal health care finally became unbearable to her. Hank won't shed tears about that, because Heather's shrill socialism makes him sick to his stomach. He's a Tea Party Republican, you see, and Heather is a #Resist Democrat. They're both American Christians, but you would never imagine that when you see their dripping disdain for one another.

Hank is a bank executive and attends an Evangelical Free Church in the suburbs. He can't fathom how anyone could call herself a Christian who believes doctors should be licensed to kill unborn babies, governments should keep religion out of schools in our "one nation under God," Americans should open our arms to immigrating terrorists, convicted criminals should be coddled, and the state should foot the bill for people who don't want to work.

Heather, in contrast, once asked her Episcopal rector, "How can anyone be both politically conservative and Christian at the same time?" She can't imagine how a Jesus person could vote against universal health care, for putting guns in dangerous hands, against housing for the homeless, and for stripping a woman's right to choose. She wonders if Hank is stupid or just bad.

Defining an in-group and an out-group is a habit

as old as humanity, as we've seen. But polarization numbers in American culture these days soar to historic levels, and the sheer intensity of Right-Left animosity, both in and outside Christianity, has grown exponentially in the past three decades. The Trump phenomenon tweaked our normal Left-Right division in 2016, but by all accounts, our animosity toward and inability to understand our political other(s) has actually continued to increase.

This chapter traces the origin of Hank and Heather's deep acrimony. These two thoughtful, well-intended people and the tribes they represent have become mortal enemies. Granted that all humans biologically incline toward the sort of in-group identification that Jonathan Haidt calls "the righteous mind," it remains for us to discover what has driven three decades of Americans to double down on division.

ALGORITHMS

Related to items you've viewed . . .
New for you . . .
Inspired by your shopping trends . . .
Recommendations for you in the Kindle Store . . .

These four simple lines, which greeted both Hank and Heather today as they opened their personalized Amazon pages, sing the anthem of our age. "We know you!" say Amazon and Google and the *New York Times* and the *Wall Street Journal* and Target and Neiman Marcus, not to mention the right panel of each one's Facebook page and all the search engines that monitor consumer intake. "We know what you've bought, so we know what you'll want to buy next." The marketing industry has been transformed in our time by brilliant algorithms that assess consumers' online activities and use them to profile our tastes.[2] It was only a matter of time before the news industry jumped on board that train.

Just as Target can profile our purchase patterns, news feeds note patterns in our news and opinion consumption. The main driver of echo-chambered consumption is this: the algorithms assume we will ever and always want to read or hear only opinions with which we are familiar and agree. Hank is a Fox News–Breitbart–*Weekly Standard* guy, so the system feeds him more and more conservative commentary. Heather frequents MSNBC, the *New York Times*, and the *Huffington Post*, so her news feed serves her a steady diet of progressive opinions. "Give the customer what she wants!" say the executives, and the computer geeks make it happen.

In a consumer age, corporations make a lot of money tracking what people choose, predicting what people will want, and then offering it to them. But as with the eight-year-old who over-orders at Cold Stone Creamery, what I want isn't always what's good for me. What I already know and like isn't necessarily what I need next.

THE NEWS WE WANT

"Jane, you ignorant slut!" began Dan Aykroyd's iconic harangues aimed at Jane Curtin, his political opposite in the classic *Saturday Night Live* sketch "Point/Counterpoint."[3] The bit matched two fictional pundits in a hilarious war of political words. It got comic traction because, in its decade, television created a new genre of commentary that pitted a liberal and a conservative, political opposites, in an ideological cage match for the sake of entertainment. The trend began in the early 1970s, with a regularly appearing *60 Minutes* segment called "Point/Counterpoint," in which the conservative columnist James Kilpatrick debated the issues of the day with liberal commentators Nicholas von Hoffman and Shana Alexander. The concept grew to a half-hour free-standing format when *Crossfire*, featuring Pat Buchanan from the Right and Tom Braden from the

Left, premiered on a Washington, DC, radio station in 1978 and grabbed excellent ratings for CNN television throughout the 1980s. Many other adaptations of the lefty-versus-righty bout have followed and escalated the polemic, in our aptly named "Age of Angertainment."[4]

The year 1996 marked a seismic change in the point-counterpoint plan. Suddenly, the cage match partisans each got their own show. Within six months of one another in that fateful year, Fox News Channel and MSNBC began broadcasting opposition news. Rupert Murdoch founded the Fox News organization with the tag line Fair and Balanced to counterweight from the Right the purportedly-neutral-but-in-his-view-liberal-leaning network news being produced by ABC, CBS, and NBC (and, after 1980, CNN). MSNBC's left-leaning identity developed gradually, but by the mid-2000s the programming had become overtly and consistently liberal.

In their two decades side-by-side in the news section of the cable dial, Fox News and MSNBC have increasingly played out the two roles that began on the "Point/Counterpoint" set two decades earlier. In its choice of news stories and its tone of commentary, Fox brings a strident and consistently conservative voice to both its news reporting and its commentary, while MSNBC reports and chatters with an increasingly unrestrained liberal voice. Each employs token opposition, the way the Harlem Globetrotters basketball team once used the hapless Washington Generals, as a lame litmus of their own brilliance.

Radio had already reached this crossroads a decade earlier, when, in 1987, the FCC repealed the Fairness Doctrine. In the four decades since 1949, that policy had required as a condition of licensure that stations (a) discuss important political issues on the air and (b) represent the conflicting views on those issues in the way they air it. The change was not abrupt—the courts had softened the doctrine through a series of decisions—but the repeal represents a landmark moment, nonetheless. Henceforth, radio stations could be unabashedly conservative or liberal. Rush Limbaugh began his wildly successful national show in one short year later, 1988, and other conservative voices followed him into the new world. Progressive radio got out of the gate more slowly, but it eventually seized the opportunity as well.

On both radio and television, the earthshaking difference between our recent Fox and MSNBC partisan screeds and their late-twentieth-century "Point/Counterpoint" forebears, came when voices from Left and Right no longer shouted at one another in the same room—or on the same channel. The archconservative and the bleeding-heart liberal no longer perform before a mixed political audience. Instead, in our time, conservative pundits play to a conservative ideal viewer, and liberal talking heads fling it to their liberal target audience. Engaged (though showy) debate has devolved into two separate pep rallies.

At least as important as their specific political tilt, cable news and, specifically, Fox News and MSNBC, interrupted a time-honored American communal custom. From the dawn of broadcast television in the Dwight Eisenhower 1950s through the middle of the Bill Clinton '90s, Americans watched essentially the same television news coverage. Those broadcasts constituted a piece of our shared cultural literacy. Some may have detected a political slant in *CBS Evening News* or *The News Hour*, but, compared to our current spectrum, those differences were relatively minor, and again, everyone talked over breakfast about the same show. Once Fox and MSNBC claimed political sides of the street, however, Americans began to process the events of their nation and world through an unabashedly partisan lens. We began in the late '90s—and especially in the George W. Bush 2000s—to choose our news.

This habit of choosing our news has received a

significant boost in recent years as news consumption has moved to the internet. More and more Americans get their news online, through their computers and mobile devices. In 2016, Pew Research Center found that fully half of Americans fifty and under get most or all of their news through electrons. Online media outlets like Breitbart on the right and Huffington Post and Slate on the left have stretched the political range even one tick further to the extremes.[5] This trend extends even further through social media, where leading personalities produce or curate the news in ways that move the extremes a couple ticks further out.[6]

This change has had a profound impact on the cohesion (or lack of same) in our communities. It's no coincidence that American levels of political polarization have mirrored almost exactly the rise in affinity group loyalties to conservative or liberal media outlets. "Political polarization is the defining feature of early 21st century American politics, both among the public and elected officials," says Carroll Daugherty of the Pew Research Center.[7] The quote summarizes an ambitious 2014 study of American political orientations. The Fox/MSNBC phenomenon has increased "party-line fidelity." By this, Pew means a consistent adherence to one political party's platform. In the two decades since the advent of the

Fox/MSNBC era, the percentage of Americans who "express consistently conservative or consistently liberal opinions" has doubled. This maps the shift in the center of gravity in each party away from the other, because it places the median beliefs of one party further at odds with the median beliefs of the other.

A second impact of the Cable News Wars and subsequent online news social-media extensions of them is a growing animosity between members of the two parties. Choosing our news has even affected how we choose our friends. We learned earlier that dislike and danger across political difference has increased in the decades since 1960. More exacting research matches the escalation with the FOX-MSNBC phenomenon. Pew's research reveals the way neighbors look at each other across fences or restaurant dining rooms or airplane aisles. According to the Pew results, between 1994 and 2014, the share of the American population who "have very unfavorable opinions" of people from the opposite political party jumped from 17 percent to 40 percent.[8] Pew also tracked our patterns of friendship and association—the classic "some of my best friends are . . ." line that we use to distance ourselves from charges of bigotry. In the two Fox/MSNBC decades, Americans have developed what Daugherty calls "ideological silos." The Pew study asked whether respondents choose friends on political criteria, and 49 percent of liberals say they seek only liberal friends, with a whopping 63 percent of conservatives searching only in conservative precincts for theirs.[9] The toxic 2016 election season surely shoved these numbers upward. We even see danger in one another's eyes. In 2014, Pew found that 27 percent of Democrats and 36 percent of Republicans "see the opposite party as a threat to the nation's well-being." This escalates difference to threat level: "one side sees safety where the other sees danger."[10]

While these changes in the habits of the American electorate surely have a hundred possible causes, the uncanny coincidence of this increase in polarization and the rise of the two partisan news channels names one central driver—especially when online news, blogs, and social media follow the same bifurcated pattern. When liberals and conservatives devour the news that repeatedly reinforces their perspective, these broadcasts shift in function from educational and informational to formational and affirmational—from an enlightening encounter with the events of the world to a pep rally that affirms and bolsters us in our preconceived way of interpreting them. Our given groupishness gloms on to politics.

THE CHURCH WE WANT

The twenty-first-century phrase for finding a place to worship in the United States is "church shopping." Faithful folk seek a church where "we feel at home." When asked why we finally land on a winner, we say something like, "I feel so comfortable there," or "I get so much out of First Church." At least one element of "feeling comfortable" in and "getting so much out of" a church is its theological and political orientation.

See if you can relate to this experience: You walk into a church on Memorial Day or the Sunday nearest the Fourth of July, and the pastors make it clear within five minutes whether you belong there or not. In a left-leaning church, Memorial Day worshippers mourn the fact of war and the greed that brought it to be; worshippers in a conservative church celebrate the heroism of the soldiers who gave the ultimate sacrifice for our nation. Liberal Independence Day sermons lean to liberation; fundies fete freedom on the Fourth. By the time the liberals have sung, "We Shall Overcome" to the conservatives' "Onward Christian Soldiers," and the liberals have read, "The one who lives by sword will die by the sword" (Matthew 26:52) and the conservatives have read, "Let everyone be subject to the governing authorities" (Romans 13:1-2)—by then you know whether you belong or not.

Most churches in our age lean Left or Right. If we Americans self-segregate politically by the news we choose, we also self-segregate through the churches we choose. Bill Bishop made this point in *The Big Sort*, as we saw in chapter 1. By again placing us with crowds who are like us, receiving messages that we like, Sunday morning sings along with the rest of our ideological week. On our generation's watch, Martin Luther King Jr.'s famous claim that "eleven o'clock on Sunday morning is the most segregated hour in America" has increasingly become true, not just racially, but theologically and politically.

Like finds like. That timeless principle of human associations needs no demonstration. We know it, not only by observing others, but through our own migratory patterns. You and I naturally hang with people of our race, socioeconomic level, religion, and so on. It's why there is a Chinatown in San Francisco; a biker bar in Sturgis, South Dakota; a cool-kid table, a goth table, and a nerd table in a middle-school cafeteria; and all the other voluntary gatherings of our lives. Academics call this tendency "homophily." In an article aptly titled "Birds of a Feather," sociologists from Duke and the University of Arizona offer a basic definition: "Homophily is the principle that a contact between similar people occurs at a higher rate than among dissimilar people."[11] Sounds right and understated!

THE COMPANY WE KEEP

Hank, our conservative banker, starts his day with a news feed that offers him Bill Kristol's *Weekly Standard* column, Charles Krauthammer's *Washington Post* piece, and some more sensational bits from Breitbart. The radio in his Escalade is set to the local Limbaugh station, so his forty-five-minute commute fortifies him for today's conversations. He arrives at a workplace that has been "coincidentally" stocked with employees from his political herd, so lunchtime conversation provides a stage for those Limbaugh lines and a few choice comments about the Democrats' latest atrocity—all to the approving amens of his colleagues. On the way home, he hits the gym, where his earbuds hitch him to Fox News on the screen above his treadmill. When he gets home, he hunkers down for some Hannity on the way to bed. Sunday morning, he'll hear a sermon on the evils of politicians and entertainers who are conspiring to stamp out Christianity.

Heather, our tech executive, lives the same day in an opposite way. She eats breakfast while reading

Gail Collins or Paul Krugman in the *New York Times*, and greets her recycling neighbors from a homogeneously liberal neighborhood as she climbs into her Prius. A Rachel Maddow podcast serenades her commute before she joins a water cooler conversation that retells the latest *Saturday Night Live* Trump slam or a riff from Bill Maher or John Oliver on the Republicans. At lunchtime, her news feed throws her *Vox* or *Huffington Post*, then she catches MSNBC on the screen above her rowing machine. Sunday's sermon will condemn global warming with the urgent tone Hank's church uses about terrorism.

Here is the key truth amid all the history and data we've traced: No one force-feeds Hank and Heather their partisan diets. They experience themselves as free agents and think they're making good choices. Their media electives may follow party lines, but their life circumstances are surely light-years away from the sort of brainwashing that leads to suicide bombings or cult membership. Hank and Heather would scoff at the suggestion that their careful control of their ideological input resembles what cult leaders do to insulate their members from dissent. But their carefully tailored echo chambers reiterate and reinforce their politics every day and incline them to despise ideas and people outside their camp. Their own religious and political slant is not the only world they know, but it's clearly the only world they want to know, and they curate intake carefully. It's no wonder their chance encounters with that other world of their political opposites produces disdain and righteous anger. "How could anyone believe that?!"

In Search of a
Better Algorithm

It's time for a new formula. Our marketing and media algorithms, along with a native draw to the path of least resistance, usher us toward sameness and affirmation. "You liked that, so we think you'll like this." "You read this, so you'll surely want to read that." They assume that we want a uniform diet of goods and input.

Now, though, imagine a different starting point. Can you picture an algorithm that expects consumers and voters to welcome challenges and variety instead of echo chambers and pep rallies? Like a nutritionist prescribing a good protein-carbohydrate balance, our new logarithm would detect what's missing in our news diet and suggest supplements. "Your last six articles have been E. J. Dionne. It's about time to read some Krauth." "You've loaded up on Hannity long enough. A moment with Mad-

dow wouldn't hurt." Imagine if the sorting mechanisms were designed to challenge our tastes and convictions and widen our intake, rather than affirming
and bolstering them and narrowing our world. Imagine a news feed designed to expose us to a wide range
of opinions and cut into biases.

The larger issue in all this is human flourishing.
It's time to challenge our culture's unproven and
unconsidered assumption that flocking with birds of
our own feather produces flourishing lives, individ-
ually and nationally. It's time for us to ask what it
would look like—how we would read and hear news,
how we would choose our neighborhoods and our
churches and our friends, how we would treat one
another—in a church and nation that could properly
be called a House United.

NOTES

1. Oxford English Living Dictionary (online), s.v. "echo chamber," http://tinyurl.com/ycbbkh5r.

2. Utpal M. Dolakia, "The Perils of Algorithm-Based Marketing," *Harvard Business Review*, June 2015, http://tinyurl.com/ybb2trxn), points out the limitations of this method, but only to help marketers refine it and become more accurately predictive of consumers' tastes.

3. For a sample of Aykroyd and Curtin's brilliant satire, see "Weekend Update: Jane, You Ignorant Slut," *Saturday Night Live*, season 4, 1979, http://tinyurl.com/jypp52q.

4. Urban Dictionary (online), s.v. "Angertainment," http://tinyurl.com/yavrsp4a.

5. Amy Mitchell, Jeffrey Gottfried, Michael Barthel, and Elisa Shearer, "Pathway to News," The Modern New Consumers, Pew Research Center, https://tinyurl.com/y8ysesvp.

6. For an in depth analysis of how social media has impacted our consumption of news, see Cass Sunstein, *#Republic: Divided Democracy in the Age of Social Media* (Princeton: Princeton University Press, 2017).

7. Carroll Doherty, "7 Things to Know about Polarization in America," *FactTank* (Pew Research Center blog), June 12, 2014, http://tinyurl.com/y7y36f52.

8. Republicans lead this race toward disfavor at 43 percent, compared with 38 percent of Democrats. Doherty, "7 Things to Know."

9. Doherty, "7 Things to Know."

10. Institute for the Advanced Studies in Culture, "Survey Finds 'Two Nations in One,'" news release, September 19, 2016, http://tinyurl.com/y75rmwse.

11. Miller McPherson, Lynn Smith-Lovin, and James M. Cook, "Birds of a Feather: Homophily in Social Networks," *Annual Review of Sociology* 27 (2001): 415, http://tinyurl.com/y8vcex9t.

5

THE DIVIDENDS
OF DIFFERENCE

Society is unity in diversity.[1]

—G. H. Mead

My theology changed on Palm Sunday morning of 2015.

No brilliant sermon, anthem, or hymn moved me, and the pastoral prayer didn't change my mind, though I'm sure all these pieces of worship rolled well. My moment of transformation came, against all odds, during the announcements. That's like having a biblical breakthrough while reading a genealogy. And yet, it happened.

Ward Brehm, a friend and longtime frequenter of African mission, ascended the chancel that morning to sell us on Opportunity International, an international micro-lending nongovernmental organization (NGO). Wayzata Community Church planned to send our Easter offering to that group, and Ward wanted to tell us why. In the middle of that mission moment, God got me. Here are Ward's words: "When I remind you that many millions of people in Africa live on one dollar per day, most of you will feel two things: pity and guilt. Both of those are understandable, even biblical responses. But I'm a businessman, so when I hear that someone in Africa lives on a dollar a day, I think, 'I gotta meet that person! I gotta find out how he does it, because I can't live on a dollar a day. This guy knows something I don't know.'"

Now, realize, I'm Mr. Inclusion. I'm the guy with one eye always scanning the room for people we leave out. I gravitate to the kid picked last on the playground, the poor sot who didn't get the party invitation, anyone who's been passed over. I sob at scenes in movies or on TV or plot turns in novels that feature left-out people getting in. (It can be embarrassing.) In fact, "Includer" is my number one of the thirty-four strengths in Gallup's Strengths-Finder list.[2]

I'm also Mr. Church Unity. I come by this trait partly through my experience as a regular attender, through years of a sort of serial ecclesial monogamy,

in congregations of fifteen different varieties of
Christianity, from conservative Baptist fundamentalism to United Church of Christ liberalism, from
high-liturgy Episcopal to no-liturgy Quaker, from
charismatic Pentecostal to staid Presbyterian, across
the map of Christianity. I emerge from that widely
various experience of church wanting Christians to
like one another more. And, as you've read already,
I know from Jesus's call to be one church (John
17:20–23) and Paul's condemnation of Corinthian
Christian division (1 Corinthians 1:11) that God
wants unity, so I try to unite Christians. Always
have. The difference in my version of inclusion from
most others is that it doesn't stop at the race-gender-
sexuality edge. My inclusion includes the non-
includers. Liberals should be kind to conservatives,
and conservatives should pray with progressives
because God wants it that way. I'm Mr. Inclusion
guy!

For years, though, I've labored to push the rock of
Christian and American inclusion and unity up the
mountain of division with a weak warrant. "Because
we should" works for some, but not for many. Also,
my existing idea that inclusion should happen for
inclusion's sake—that it's a God-given duty—can
easily, accidentally conduce to condescension.
When God calls us or compassion compels us to

include all people, we can too easily wax arrogant. "We're such good and faithful and enlightened sorts, we'll even let *you* into our church." Even stronger in our present context is our temptation to feel superior to those other so-called Christians or citizens who are too judgmental and callous to open their doors.

Ward's words undermined that false superiority. Suddenly I lost my power in the inclusion exchange. In that moment, I became the guy who needs help from people I don't yet know. My church became a group that needs that sort of help. Ward's words changed our congregation's question from "Whom should we include?" to "Whom do we need?" A church built on Ward's question about dollar-a-day Africans would stop often to ask, "Who are we missing around this table?"

Played out as a philosophy, this approach to outreach changes everything, not just for Christian division, but for American polarization. It transfers inclusion from the category of duty to the realm of enlightened self-interest. During these last two decades, as we've seen, with widening divisions all around us, more and more Americans (and Christian Americans) have come to believe that our nation or our church would be better off without "them." "They" are the problem, "they" are the nuisance, and "they" are the danger. Without "them," we could (if we're progressives) feed the poor, help the sick, and do the things a nation ought to do for one another. Or (if we're conservatives), we could pay off the national debt, defend our borders, restore morality, and unshackle free enterprise. Or (if we're Trumpians), we could return to simpler, pre-pluralism days, when everyone spoke the same language and believed in the same God. Things would finally be good, if we could just get rid of "them."

In Christian circles, being rid of "them" makes sense when progressives can't picture a single way that a biblical literalist might help us get it right, or conservatives have no idea how questioning the Bible's passages on homosexuality could be useful to our congregation's discernment.

But what if we need "them"? What if there are things a liberal doesn't know that a conservative just gets? What if a progressive could bring just the right challenge to a theologically traditional assumption? If my marriage featured two of me, I'd be in trouble, and I think Liz, my wife, would say the same thing about two of her. As competitive as each of us is, neither of us really wants to win every debate, because we know how God uses our personality differences to build something better than either of us could have concocted on our own. It's good for a lavish spender to have a fiscal conservative to temper his profligate ways; and it's good for a careful hoarder to have someone to push her toward some risk-taking. A lot of good marriages are built on difference.

Ward Brehm's perspective suggests that all of life is that way—that all of us would gain by asking, "What voice are we missing at this table?" Hank and Heather ought to hold their nose for a moment and get a cup of coffee together—not out of duty, but because they need one another in order to get it right. Wisconsin farmers know something Chicago urbanites don't, and vice versa. Pure left-wing policies and pure right-wing policies lack the wisdom of the other side. Inclusion is not just faithful. Designed by a God who loves humanity, it naturally becomes a way of getting and being better.

Business and military leaders know this Brehm bonus.

VARIETY MAKES MONEY

The first episode of the television series *Mad Men* aired in 2007 to critical acclaim and excellent ratings. The series casts our eyes back to a time (the early 1960s) when white men from the same colleges, wearing the same style of business suits and living in the same neighborhoods, ran the world. The communications professionals who make up Sterling Cooper Draper Pryce do their white, male eastern prep school best to compete with and defeat their competition for marketing contracts. Lucky for them, the competition hires the same demographic. The series received critical acclaim at least partly for its historically accurate depiction of American corporate culture in the early 1960s.

Over the half century since the *Mad Men* epoch, firms and corporate teams have added brown hues and XX chromosomes to their mix, but we've already seen that a leftover form of discrimination hurts some businesses. The Stanford study we perused earlier found that 80 percent of would-be bosses (both Democrats and Republicans), faced with equally skilled and experienced applicants, selected their own in-party candidate.[3] The irony about that is that business is waking up faster than politics, religion, or higher education to the truth that, not just ethnic and gender mixes, but also ideological diversity helps their bottom line.

Those in high corporate places may not pay a social price for political prejudice—it's in vogue to segregate!—but an increasing lot of research suggests that they do pay a financial price. Here's the problem with the *Mad Men*/same-as-us strategy: birds-of-a-feather hiring practices hurt productivity.

Firms that, like Sterling Cooper Draper Pryce, sort for racial and gender sameness, or employers who consciously or unconsciously hire for political sameness, disadvantage themselves in the marketplace. By recruiting people just like themselves to staff their teams, they lose a key element needed for success in problem solving and idea generation: multiple perspectives.

"The right perspective can make a difficult problem simple," writes University of Michigan economist Scott Page. "Perspectives . . . create super-additive effects. They can be combined to form ever more perspectives." Page shows that hiring people, even highly intelligent people, who approach a problem in the same way does not multiply the opportunities for breakthrough. In fact, he'll challenge your high-IQ sameness with a lower-IQ diversity any day. His reason? "Diverse teams make better mousetraps."[4] Another researcher puts it more bluntly: "Decades of research by organizational scientists, psychologists, sociologists, economists and demographers shows that socially diverse groups (that is, those with a diversity of race, ethnicity, gender and sexual orientation) are more innovative than homogeneous groups."[5] Researchers have recently added ideology and conservative versus liberal orientation to that list of diverse perspectives.

Bottom-line advantage motivates business leaders much more effectively than affirmative-action quotas have. "In today's increasingly diverse, global, interconnected business world, diversity and inclusion is no longer just 'the right thing to do.' It is a core to leadership competency and central to the success of business. . . . [It] not only leads to a more productive, innovative corporate culture, but also to better engagement with customers and clients."[6] The title of this quotation's source tells the story: *The Inclusion Dividend: Why Investing in Diversity and Inclusion Pays Off.*

I've emphasized the advantage of idea diversity for companies, but widening the range of contacts also advances individual careers. Citing Michael Simmons acknowledges the countervailing attraction of sameness. Insider groups know each other's codes, complete simple tasks more easily, and generally feel more comfortable. That's why "most people spend their careers in closed networks."[7] For all these tempting attributes, though, sameness does not deliver for the career minded. "People in open networks have unique challenges and opportunities. Because they're part of multiple groups, they have unique relationships, experiences, and knowledge that other people in their groups don't." As a result, people who risk venturing into open networks reap career-enhancing rewards: a more accurate view of the world, the ability to control the timing of information sharing, the ability to translate or connect between groups, and—here's the brass ring—more breakthrough ideas. To drive the argument home, Simmons produces Steve Jobs as his poster boy.[8]

We should avoid getting too pat or sloppy here. Diversity is not uncomplicated. The best books on business applications properly take pains not to make diversity an absolute. They clarify the specific tasks and functions that benefit from including difference. Forefront among these are problem solving and prediction of results. Because corporate success relies heavily on those two functions, the advantage is great. But those same studies caution that, not surprisingly, both cultural and ideological diversity can also divide a working group. In these polarized times, disagreement about political matters can initially hinder team building and undermine trust between colleagues.

This last fact confronts leaders with an important choice: they could either continue hiring sameness or teach their people how to capitalize on their difference. The latter requires a major culture change—the very change I advocate in this book. That's why, despite the potential conflicts, because the profit motive drives businesses and a growing body of research shows that diverse teams ultimately make more money, I expect the corporate world to diversify its teams more and more in years to come.

Variety Captures the Flag

If business leaders increasingly choose their diversity, military units are stuck with it. The US Army, Navy, Air Force, and Marines play the matchmaker to thousands of arranged marriages, throwing soldiers into squads and units they don't choose to meet leaders who did not choose them. To make this more difficult, the military population has become one of the most racially, economically, educationally, religiously, and politically diverse collections of people in the United States in our time.[9] Yet, these thrown-together units continue to accomplish amazing feats of collaboration, and military teams often become closer than family for the soldiers. Inquiring polarized minds want to know how they do it.

I lead a nonprofit initiative called House United, which is devoted to "bringing people together across difference for the common good." In cities around the nation, we form local teams who find creative ways to accomplish this goal. In March 2017, the House United team in Phoenix, Arizona, came up with a new way of showing what we mean. This team invited six experienced active-duty and retired soldiers on to a stage and simply asked them to tell their stories. These six differed significantly from one another, ranging in rank from colonel to grunt, in ethnicity from Latino to African American to Caucasian, in religion from a devout conservative Christian pastor to a progressive churchgoer to a disinterested agnostic, in age from twenty-something to sixty-something, and in educational level from a high-school dropout to a Cambridge University alum. (The panel ended up all-male, because the female officer we had invited was forced to cancel at the last minute due to illness.) They also differed politically across red and blue lines. These soldiers, so wildly different from one another, nonetheless spoke one consistent theme: their military experience taught them to receive help from sources they would formerly have dismissed as useless.

One sergeant shared his strategy for leading diverse squads: "We never know what hand we're going to get dealt. But each squad or unit has to move pretty quickly to discover who can do what." He continued, "No matter how motley the crew, I'd tell them, 'Bring what you got to the table. We're gonna need it!'" In this leader's experience, diverse military groups accomplish more complex tasks more effectively than their more homogeneous counterparts.

An expert mechanic proudly told of a time when he managed to restore a destitute troop transport vehicle almost all the way back to full health. But there was a wrinkle. Just before the vehicle sparked to life, he got stuck. He simply couldn't figure out how to stop air from escaping out the back end of the system. He tried everything he could imagine, but remained stumped—and a little desperate, because the mission depended on him not being stumped. When our mechanic ran out of options and asked for help, a young nobody from the unit stepped forward, holding up a simple part—the thing you and I use to put air in our tires at gas stations—and asked, "Will this do?" They were on the road in minutes. The mechanic looked at the problem through the eyes of a mechanic. The grunt looked at it through the eyes of a guy who had a lot of flat tires. Problem solved.

Several soldiers also shared how their encounters with difference changed them. One African American officer who is a Christian from the Alabama Bible Belt ran headlong into a Muslim from New York, and what started as a brief dinner conversation went on for long hours. They're still friends. One African American officer told of a white man from

North Dakota who had never seen a black man before boot camp, and even touched his skin out of curiosity. All told of friendships forged across lines of difference. They filled the hour with stories like this and at the end assured us that we would hear the same thing from other cross-sections of the service. Anecdotes and a growing body of statistics bear out the asset that diverse perspectives are to military success.[10]

The voice of Scott Page rings from offstage. Multiplying perspectives multiplies possible solutions, and when you're in the business of completing missions, sometimes the guy who remembers having a flat tire can get you home. Michael Simmons's voice chimes in, too. If you want to grow personally, sameness won't get you there as fast. The military introduced these people to exotic characters from different spheres, a network they still access both personally and professionally. The military taught them that difference is an asset.

Perspective diversity makes better ideas. Business and the military are waking up to the advantages of staffing difference. But the leaders of our churches, academies, and government continue to operate on segregated, winner-take-all models, unable to imagine that their ideological counterparts could contribute anything of value. Despite evidence and common sense that tell us diverse perspectives help us, these three institutions, which significantly shape our culture, continue to hold a "sameness is best" policy. We've seen the dismal results of that insistence in the breakdown of Christian communities, the problems with free speech on our campuses, and the stalemates that plague our government.

THE THEOLOGY OF DESIGNED DIFFERENCE

Ironically, the patron saint for the power of diversity is the apostle Paul. In spite of his *persona non grata* status among many diversity-prizing Christians in our time, when Paul paints Christian community, difference splashes all over the canvas. In 1 Corinthians 12, Paul tells a living-room-sized gathering of Christians that God gave them their wisdom, knowledge, faith, and their ability to heal, perform miracles, prophesy, discern spirits, speak in tongues, and interpret those tongues. Then he tells them why: "To each one the manifestation of the Spirit is given for the common good" (12:7, NIV). Christians have for a couple of thousand years seen the "gifts of the Spirit" as what we are naturally good at: strengths, talents, skills, natural endowments. That is true, as far as it goes. Wisdom is something some

113

people have more of than others, and crediting God for it is a good idea. Since Paul never claimed to build a comprehensive list, though, you and I would likely even throw a few more items on the list: musical talent, physical strength, rhetorical skills, a good listening ear, and others. We can easily imagine how God could use all of these strengths "for the common good."

Theological and political ideas also belong on this list. As far as I can see in the literature on 1 Corinthians 12, in our nearly two thousand year history, we Christians have never even dabbled with the thought that Paul could be talking about our different ways of defining God, the human, the good to be done, etc.—different beliefs or doctrines. But we should. Researchers have shown that ideological orientation may be innate. By tracking twins who've been raised in different contexts, sociologists have for decades sought to isolate genetics as the significant variable in personality types. Lately some have helpfully shifted their emphasis to the conservative-liberal axis of personality, with fascinating results.[11]

First, we define terms. As we do, I recommend caution, because the language can reveal the definer's bias. As an example, James Fowler's widely read book, *The Stages of Faith,* puts "conformity to authority" (a conservative trait) at the relatively immature stage 3 level, while the nirvana of stage 6 faith is "universalizing" (a liberal trait). Placing one-self at the pinnacle of existence rings of neither humility nor accuracy. It reminds me of historical-Jesus scholars who conveniently discover that Jesus was a latte-sipping, *New York Times* reading liberal, just like them. Because the halls of academe abound with progressives, left-leaning bias is common in the academic definitions of "conservative" and "liberal."

One scholar who avoids these definitional pitfalls is Dana Carney, whose work encapsulates seventy-five years of this research. This work isolates two test traits that skew to opposite political approaches: openness to new experiences, on the one hand and conscientiousness, on the other. Survey research probes these two orientations by measuring sub-jects' readiness to embrace novel activities and diverge from valued traditions, including informal taboos. The team then reports a relatively value-neutral description of the two orientations in "The Secret Lives of Liberals and Conservatives." Carney writes, "Liberals are more open-minded, creative, curious, and novelty seeking, whereas Conserva-tives are more orderly, conventional, and better organized."[12]

I hope you've noticed that these studies place political "orientation" among our biologically given traits. Researchers have more to do, and the question remains live, but a growing wave of discoveries compellingly link personality traits with political predispositions.[13] I choose the word *orientation* carefully here, because that term and its causes—nature or nurture—lie at the center of the homosexuality debate that has divided Christians for four decades. By using the term, I am suggesting that the predilection to challenge the notion that homosexual orientation is a biologically given orientation to sexuality may itself be prompted by a biologically given conservative orientation to life. Mind-bending!

Tracing our conservative-liberal tendencies to biological causes obviously carries theological implications. Let's try an experiment. Imagine for a moment that God's "variety of gifts" does include a naturally conservative disposition and a naturally liberal one—that God has made us theologically and politically different from one another. First, that would challenge our own current Christian tendency and societal dysfunction that sees its opposites as, at best, an inconvenience and, at worst, useless. Second, it would replace that winner-take-all competition we've chronicled with a generative, communal desire to capitalize on the merits of both leftish and rightish orientations in the same way we welcome artistic people, organizational heads, and contemplative sorts as gifts to a congregation.

To picture how necessary this variety is to a working human community, the apostle Paul uses the analogy of a human body: "Who could hear if she were all eyes? And who could smell if he were all ears?" And that's not even to mention legs for mobility or hands to feed mouths. Paul's point is clear: communities don't work if everyone's good at the same things.

Jonathan Haidt offers this Pauline point in a different form for our times: "If one side controls everything, then the whole country's going to go to hell in very predictable ways. We're all these moralistic creatures who are using our reasoning to support our side, and the other side is not evil, the other side does not hate America and want to destroy it. Both sides are persuing different morals, and we actually need elements of both in a society."[14] In short, sometimes we need our religious or political or moral opposites to save us from ourselves.

In his powerful book *Tribe*, Sebastian Junger writes, "The most alarming rhetoric comes out of the dispute between liberals and conservatives, and it's a dangerous waste of time because they're both right."[15] Junger illustrates his claim with one example: the Left-Right difference on welfare and entitlement programs. Junger says American conservatives are evolutionarily correct to worry about the able-bodied and able-minded who would live off the dole. And American liberals are evolutionarily correct to represent the needs of the vulnerable. Both positions have credible evolutionary roots, and their competing interests originally gave birth to the two-party system. Throughout American history, the tense conversation between those two interests has produced brilliant compromises. The abdication of that conversation leaves us stalled.

My point is simple: things could be otherwise. While polarization may seem inevitable to us, there was a time when it was not. Remember that the change captured in our alarming statistic—the rise from 4.5 to 43 percent of parents being worried that their son or daughter might marry into the opposite political party—happened in five decades. The statistics that display this chasm are all relatively new. We could choose to process our differences differently, and the apostle Paul, along with front-edge business and military leaders, join my friend Ward Brehm in suggesting that we should. In fact, maybe these advantages of diverse community explain well why Jesus prayed "that they all may be one." It's time to ask how.

NOTES

1. George H. Mead, "National-Mindedness and International-Mindedness," *International Journal of Ethics* 39, no. 4 (1929): 385–407.

2. *StrengthsFinder* and *Strengthsfinder 2.0* are Gallup-commissioned tools that help management teams to identify their specific human resources. Participants take a battery of tests that sort thirty-four specific "strengths" from strongest to weakest. Tom Rath and Donald Clifton, *Strengths Finder 2.0* (New York: Gallup Press, 2007).

3. Shanto Iyengar and Sean J. Westwood, "Fear and Loathing across Party Lines: New Evidence on Group Polarization" (unpublished paper, Stanford University, June 2014), http://tinyurl.com/yd8jbqn3.

4. Scott E. Page, *The Difference: How the Power of Diversity Creates Better Groups, Firms, Schools, and Societies* (Princeton: Princeton University Press, 2008), 50.

5. Katherine W. Phillips, "How Diversity Makes Us Smarter," *Scientific American*, October 1, 2014, http://tinyurl.com/y8mc5m5t.

6. Mark Kaplan and Mason Donovan, *The Inclusion Dividend: Why Investing in Diversity and Inclusion Pays Off* (Brookline, MA: Bibliomotion, 2013).

7. Sociologists call this birds-of-a-feather approach homophily, and they emphasize its costs. One writes, "Homophily limits people's social worlds in a way that has powerful implications for the information they receive, the attitudes they form, and the interactions they experience." Miller McPherson et al., "Birds of a Feather: Homophily in Social Networks," *Annual Review of Sociology* 27 (2001): 415.

8. Michael Simmons, "The No. 1 Predictor of Career Success according to Network Science," *Forbes*, January 15, 2015, http://tinyurl.com/y9uhnurv.

9. The US Military is 60 percent white, 17 percent black, 12 percent Hispanic, 4 percent Asian, and 7 percent other. Educational diversity has risen also. Political diversity, though present, has not been quantified in the same way, because most people do not count it a demographic category. For a good run at the data we have, see Kim Parker, et al., "6 Facts about the US Military and Its Changing Demographics," Pew Research Center, April 13, 2017, http://tinyurl.com/ybvoyge6.

10. The increasing diversity of the military has not been uncontroversial. Most claims of diversity's advantages are anecdotal at this point, but the stories are multiplying. For evidence of the ongoing debate, see Carl Forsling, "Why the Military Needs Diversity," *Task and Purpose*, April 28, 2015, http://tinyurl.com/ybsq7g3c.

11. Lizzie Buchen offers an accessible summary in "Biology and Ideology: The Anatomy of Politics," *Nature*, October 24, 2012, http://tinyurl.com/y8hn3ccs. Nicholas Martin and colleagues supply a more technical study in N. G. Martin, L. J. Eaves, A. C. Heath, R. Jardine, L. M. Feingold, and H. J. Eysenck, "Transmission of Social Attitudes," *Proceedings of the National Academy of Sciences of the United States of America* 83, no. 12 (1986): 4364–68.

12. Dana R. Carney, John T. Jost, Samuel D. Gosling, and Jeff Potter, "The Secret Lives of Liberals and Conservatives: Personality Profiles, Interaction Styles, and the Things They Leave Behind," *Political Psychology* 29, no. 6 (2008): 807–40, http://tinyurl.com/yb2t76e2.

13. See, for example, Avi Tuschman's piece "Can Your Genes Predict Whether You'll Be a Conservative or a Liberal?," *Atlantic*, October 24, 2013, http://tinyurl.com/yaqtf8uh. He features Jack and Jeanne Block's longitudinal study, "Nursery School Personality and Political Orientation Two Decades Later," *Journal of Research in Personality.* 40 (2005): 734–49. http://tinyurl.com/yaaxexne.

14. Bill Weir, "Is a Conservative or Liberal Born or Made?," *Nightline*, October 11, 2012, http://tinyurl.com/ybbp73mo.

15. Sebastian Junger, *Tribe: On Homecoming and Belonging* (New York: Hachette, 2016), 35.

6

MEETING
THROUGH
MISSION

True friends face in the same direction, toward
common projects, interests, goals.
—C. S. Lewis, *The Four Loves*

Once upon a time, a prosperous Christian congregation in Dallas, Texas, sought a worthy mission by
which to serve the world with its considerable gifts.
After vetting several good options, their collective
discernment led them to a beautiful project. They
discovered along the Mexican border of Texas a vast
population of children who needed and wanted education, and a ready stable of teachers willing to edu-
cate them, but no safe shelter in which teachers and

learners could meet and work. The church heard in that moment God's call to build schoolhouses along the border. They decided to paint each building a beautiful blue that would signal to the children, "Come hither and learn." They built and painted. A mission had begun.

In time, this mission of schoolhouse building and painting grew and drew the attention of news outlets across Texas. One day, when it hit the evening news on a Houston TV broadcast, a church leader in that city happened to be watching and recognized an opportunity for his own congregation. After discerning with the proper people, he telephoned the Dallas church and asked if his flock might collaborate with them in this beautiful mission. Soon two churches were building and painting blue schoolhouses on the border, and more children got to learn in the shelter of their own beautiful new classrooms.

This story is heartwarming, but it hardly seems unusual or dramatic. Christian churches occasionally do find our way to joining forces for good, and telling about it is the kind of thing local news editors do, in order to leave viewers with warm feelings as they end their half-hour broadcasts.

The story becomes strange and wonderful, though, when we learn the identity of the story's protagonists. In the polarized contemporary American church, this was a moment of astonishing Christian unity. The Cathedral of Hope in Dallas was a growing, thriving congregation with an Open and Affirming identity[1] and a large gay population, the very epitome of Progressive Christianity. Prosperity and generosity had prompted the leaders of COH to seek a significant mission. After discernment, in 2001 they undertook the Little Blue Schools project. They succeeded so resoundingly that a leader from a Houston Southern Baptist church caught wind of the story and placed a call.

A little context: Then, as now, the Southern Baptist Convention stated its position on homosexual orientation and behavior simply: "The Bible condemns it as a sin. . . . The same redemption available to all sinners is available to homosexuals."[2] At that time, Southern Baptist pastoral work with gay men and lesbian woman took the form of reparative therapy, by which they hoped God might transform the gay or lesbian person's orientation into heterosexuality.[3]

To understate, a welcome-the-gays church and a repair-the-gays church do not usually hang out together. But these Southern Baptists didn't initially know about the Cathedral of Hope's identity. They only knew the shape of their mission to Mexican children, so they jumped in and joined the blue-schoolhouse-building work. By the time the builders and painters grasped the extent of their differences, they already had the momentum of mission and relationship, so they kept painting. A fundamentalist church and a rainbow church building and painting together to serve their needy world—in our day, that is miraculous!

When Jesus prayed "that they all may be one" (John 17:20), maybe this is the sort of thing he meant.

FINDING SOMETHING BETTER TO DO

The odds stacked themselves against our shared-mission miracle. In the past three decades, Christians have left their congregations, congregations have left their denominations, and whole worldwide denominations have come apart at the seams over the issue of gay and lesbian membership and marriage. At the moment of this collaboration between two opposites on the issue, homosexuality had just begun to contend with abortion as the most divisive issue in Christendom. Churches like the ones in my example are supposed to quietly disdain or even shout ridicule at one another across the airwaves, not go on mission trips together.

This very red church and this very blue church

continued hammering schoolhouse walls instead of one another because they momentarily changed their priorities. For one brilliant moment, in the midst of our American church culture wars, the well-being of Mexican kids looked even more important to one progressive church and one fundamentalist church than their own quibbles and quarrels.

We can grab an important insight from the Little Blue Schools project: to engage another Christian or church across a wide gap in beliefs, churches and individual Christians can make a good beginning meeting through mission. In one episode of NBC's award-winning television series (and now a Netflix fixture), *The West Wing*, the fictional Democratic president, Jed Bartlet, cultivates an unexpected ally from across the aisle, Republican Senator Max Lobell. When they sit down, the president proclaims,

BARTLET
You know what we're doing here, right?

LOBELL
We're going to talk about soft money.

BARTLET
We're going to do more than talk about it.

LOBELL
Okay.

BARTLET
We agree on nothing, Max.

LOBELL
Yes, sir.

BARTLET
Education, guns, drugs, school prayer, gays, defense spending, taxes, you name it, we disagree.

LOBELL
You know why?

BARTLET
'Cause I'm a lily-livered, bleeding-heart, liberal, egg head, communist.

LOBELL
Yes, sir. And I'm a gun-totin', redneck son-of-a-bitch.

BARTLET
Yes, you are.

LOBELL

We agree on that.

BARTLET

We also agree on campaign finance.

LOBELL

Yes, sir.

BARTLET

So, Max.

LOBELL

Yes, sir?

BARTLET

Let's work together on campaign finance.[4]

When those blue schoolhouses needed builders, the Cathedral of Hope and the Southern Baptists from Houston agreed on very little. But they both loved those kids, so they kept on pounding and painting together for them.

I have a guess at one of the things that made the kids even more compelling than the things that should have kept these two churches apart. I'll bet that UCC church in Dallas and that Southern Baptist church in Houston both learned the value of those kids from the same source: the sheep and the goats taught them.

Near the end of his ministry, in the Gospel of Matthew, Jesus pictures for his disciples the very end of time, when the Son of Man will gather all the nations together and assess their lives. In the dramatic world of the story, the assessor is a king on a throne who divides all humanity into two groups with one important commonality and one important difference. Sheep and goats share a single common experience: both groups have encountered needy people, whom Jesus calls "the least of these, my brothers and sisters." They've both met people who are hungry, thirsty, strangers, naked, sick, and imprisoned. The two groups part ways, though, in their response to need. Sheep have fed, given drink, welcomed, clothed, and visited. Goats have done nothing. That difference determines their ultimate destiny: sheep get the right-hand side during the chat and eternal bliss afterward; goats are on the left and get everlasting fire. The story stops us up short.

The Houston Southern Baptists and the Cathedral of Hope had two things in common: they both listened to Jesus's story, and they both wanted to be sheep. They read the story differently, I would imagine—from different-looking Bibles (floppy leather and gilt-paged versus stock pulpit Bible), in a different translation (New International Version in Houston, New Revised Standard Version in Dallas), with possibly a different point of emphasis (at least one eye expectantly on Jesus's second coming in Houston, one eye questioning Jesus's punishment of the goats in Dallas). But they both read the story, and they both loved Jesus, and Jesus said helping those kids actually meant helping him, so they both scanned their landscape to find "the least of these." That's how mission begins, and that leads us straight to their third common bond: when they looked for "the least," their eyes ultimately fixed on Mexican children who needed an education (aka "those kids"). In other words, in scripture they found something better to do.

Meeting at the Bible

Raise your hand if you expected the Bible to bring a progressive church and a fundamentalist church together. Christians have spilled infidels' and heretics' blood because of the Bible. Families, small groups, congregations, and denominations have split over the Bible. When Luther defied the Roman Catholic Church, he held up his Bible, and most of the denominations around the world that followed

Luther's restart began because someone interpreted the Bible differently than someone else. Some have even summarized the twentieth- and twenty-first-century fundamentalist-liberal and evangelical-progressive controversies as a "Battle for the Bible."[5]

Different ways of reading the Bible divide people in our time. Consider Leviticus 18–20. The past decade of our American culture wars have partly played out on the battlefield of these three chapters. Homosexuality and immigration would make any short list of issues that have recently divided the American electorate, and these chapters of Leviticus speak to both. Conservatives on the issue produce Leviticus 18:22 and 20:13, two of the Bible's five verses that expressly condemn some form of homosexual behavior.[6] "Do not have sexual relations with a man as one does with a woman; that is detestable," says 18:22, and 20:13 names the consequences: "If a man has sexual relations with a man as one does with a woman, both of them have done what is detestable. They are to be put to death; their blood will be on their own heads" (NIV). In chorus, many conservative congregations across America shout their "Amen!" to these verses. Conservative cake makers won't build wedding cakes for gay couples because of these verses. Marriage amendments have passed because of these verses. "God's will is clear, right there on the page."

In contrast, in a twenty-first-century American debate about immigration, many of these same Bible-loving conservative Christians conveniently jump right over Leviticus 19. Many pastors in those Leviticus 18 and 20 churches[7] tend not to preach or teach or placard Leviticus 19:33–34. Instead, the chorus of "Amen!" you hear after reading it resounds from liberal churches. Equally black-letter as the ones that flank it, this law demands, "When an alien resides with you in your land, you shall not oppress the alien. The alien who resides with you shall be to you as the citizen among you; you shall love the alien as yourself, for you were aliens in the land of Egypt: I am the Lord your God" (NRSV). American Christians who support open borders can wave their Bibles, too. They read the nineteenth chapter of Leviticus but won't come within miles of 18 and 20.

The Bible divides Left and Right, liberal and fundamentalist, and a special kind of hypocrisy drives the division. Once, as I suffered another of the US church's denominational battles over the issue of gay and lesbian ordination, I spotted a sign in the hands of a liberal advocate: "Selective Literalism Is Idolatry." She intended her sign to undermine conservative support from scripture on the issue of gay and lesbian marriage, and the sign actually speaks truth. But her interest was partisan, as she waved it at those damned conservatives. I could easily picture that very same sign waver at the next synod meeting, when the agenda moves to immigration, waving a "Leviticus 19 Forever!" placard. Selective literalism is idolatry both ways. The age-old pulpit joke still has it right: "Most people use the Bible the way a drunk uses a lamppost: more for support than for illumination." Our righteous minds have already set their course, and we're looking for ammunition. "The Bible as Ammunition" is probably not the purpose for which God intended that inspired book.

With all that said, my portrayal of a virtual Left-Right parity on scriptural engagement is misleading. To illustrate the discrepancy, come with me on an imagination excursion. You're driving along the street of your town or city on a Sunday morning. You see all the usual neighborhoods and street signs. Then you begin to see people walking toward a church building, carrying Bibles under their arms. They're thick ones. They look tattered from use. What sort of church do you imagine you're passing?

Most people would answer that, if people are toting Bibles, it must be a Southern Baptist church or an Evangelical Free church or a Saddleback/Willow Creek/North Point/Open Door sort of nondenominational church. You pretty much know it's an evangelical or fundamentalist church. Those are the people with well-worn Bibles, after all. They mark them during sermons and then read them again at home. It's part of the culture. On the other hand, that doesn't happen very often in progressive churches.

Some from those left-leaning churches would respond with the defense, "We just read the Bible differently!" But my experience agrees with Pew Research findings that progressives just read the Bible a lot less. The Pew study found that twice as many Evangelicals as progressives read the Bible at least once a week—60 percent, versus 30 percent.[8] Beyond frequency, Evangelicals have a different relationship with scripture than progressives do. Clearly, if Machen's Christian Right and Fosdick's Christian Left have finally parted ways, citing "irreconcilable differences," the conservatives got the Bible in the divorce decree.

There are legitimate reasons for this. Progressive Christians often experienced the literalist reading of the rising Christian Right in the 1970s and '80s as damaging. The public face of strong claims for the Bible has often taken the form of harsh judgment, as when conservative Christian leaders Jerry Falwell and Pat Robertson interpreted the terrorist bombings of 9/11/01 as divine judgment on those who are "throwing God out of the public schools . . . abortionists . . . feminists, and the gays and lesbians," among other abominations.[9]

The progressives had and have a point. Bible-waving judgment does prevail in some circles on the Right, leaving bruised people in its wake. But in response, progressives have often distanced themselves from the Bible itself, rather than from a way of reading it. As a result of this progressive retreat from reading, many people perceive the Bible as a conservative Christian book—a misunderstanding that perpetuates the disparity.

When progressives throw the baby of the Bible out with the bathwater of one way of reading it, everybody loses. The Left loses a central source of guidance and spiritual succor. When the popular Christian writer and speaker Rachel Held Evans departed her conservative church, she blogged her reasons, which resonated with many progressives—the subordination of women, undue focus on sex as sin, an aversion to questions and doubt, a political uniformity on the Right, and other things like this. But when she visited mainline churches, Evans found the experience lacking in another way:

> While there is much I love and appreciate about mainline denominations, when I visit, I always

leave feeling like something's missing. I miss that evangelical fire-in-the-belly that makes people talk about their faith with passion and conviction. I miss the familiarity with scripture and the intensive Bible studies. I miss the emphasis on cultivating a personal spirituality. I miss sermons that step on a few toes. *I am speaking in gross generalizations here*, but in my experience, going from evangelicalism to the mainline can feel a bit like going from one extreme to the other.[10]

We lose something essential when our relationship with scripture declines.

The Right pays a toll, too. This progressive departure from the scriptures undermines the prospect of cross-difference conversation. In the terms of the last chapter, when the progressive wing of Christianity withdraws from the Bible it abdicates its role in the wider Christian discussion. This, in turn, hurts the larger discernment processes of Christ's church by taking away whatever we would call the checks and balances of Left and Right. When a progressive politician names Jonah as a New Testament book or a preacher prefaces his Benjamin Franklin quote with "as the Bible says" or a Christian leader just argues her point from pop psychology or a Gandhi line, without even nodding to relevant biblical passages, the evangelical loses interest, the progressive loses credibility, and the Left-Right conversation gets harder—and less likely.

I have a simple idea. Let's read the Bible together. Let's reverse the MSNBC–versus–Fox News trend by bringing Christians from Left and Right around the same table to read scripture. Once we've met one another through mission, let's have UCC–Southern Baptist Bible studies, where we find our way to the rich diversity of scriptural voices. To accomplish this, progressives will have to raise our game a bit (gulp, big leather Bibles under our arms . . .), and conservatives will have to open our ears long enough to welcome additional perspectives. But let's do what it takes to read Leviticus 18, 19, and 20 and those other passages that divide us, sitting around the same table.

If an Evangelical-progressive Bible fest sounds outlandish and impossible to you, a look at the rabbis will give you hope.

HELP FROM THE RABBIS

The ancient Jewish rabbis and their descendants through the ages can help us bridge our Christian divide. The leaders of Judaism throughout history have demonstrated that a community with both strongly held and conflicting interpretations can coexist and thrive together around scripture. They have agreed to disagree, on the rationale that the conversation itself is redemptive. Rabbis have debated and vehemently disagreed for twenty-five hundred years, yet somehow the conversation continues. From Hillel and Shammai in the first century, forward through Maimonides in the Middle Ages, and onward through to the present, rabbinic debate has featured extreme ideological opposites. Hillel insisted that a man should be able to divorce his wife for doing nothing worse than burning the toast, and Shammai argued that infidelity is the only valid warrant for divorce. In fact, Hillel and Shammai disagreed on almost everything. And Hillel and Shammai have their line of descendants. Rabbinic debate can be fierce, but it continues in community.

Here's the rabbis' secret: the key to the relatively harmonious continuation of rabbinic discussion, despite strong disagreement, is an attitude about ideas and intentions. A tractate of the Talmud provides the poetic rationale: "Any disagreement for the sake of heaven shall be established in the end. What is a disagreement for the sake of heaven? The disagreement between Hillel and Shammai" (Pirke

Avot 5:17). Our generation has lost this insight that an oppositional argument may be well intended and serve a blessed purpose. We uncharitably imagine that anyone who disagrees with us is either evil or stupid. The rabbinic notion of "a disagreement for heaven's sake" sounds veritably redemptive next to our suspicious, cynical ways.

One twenty-first-century Jewish writer reflects on our encouraging Talmud passage in this way: "Judaism is not a 'winner takes all' system. From very early days, our sages recognized that even two good and wise people with good intentions might come to different conclusions. Though in the end we must choose, the fact that we remember Shammai [even as we choose to follow Hillel's practices] reminds us to be humble in those choices, and to recognize that others who choose differently may still be acting for the sake of heaven."[11] Hillel and Shammai and their spiritual offspring disagree often, but the rabbis agree that the Book is at the center of their argument. And they have a native trust that their scrimmage, even with its confrontations, is a heavenly one that will ultimately produce heavenly results. They agree about the Book—not on what it means, necessarily, but on its primacy in forming their world.

HOPE FOR TOMORROW

Friends, we can do this! Here's a bold claim in a postmodern age: we need now more than ever a Christian canon that all Christians read. As cable television and online outlets have fragmented our culture's news intake and a decentralized university curriculum has fragmented our learning, the broader culture suffers from having no common, core experience. For Christians, Bible can be that meeting place once again—even as we disagree about it. When we arrive there, we will find a much more complex world than the Bible's reputation pictures. We'll find ancient Israelites arguing over whether they ought to have a king over them or not, Paul and James arguing over whether faith or works saves us, one author holding high the hope that God saves us from hell then, and another calling us to do justice now. In the Bible, there's room for our Christian Right and our Christian Left

The Bible is a big tent book, and once we discover that fact, we can find our way to one another through a small man who built a big boat on dry land because he heard what he swore was God's voice (Genesis 6–8); an aging, childless couple who had to explain to their neighbors that God had ordered both the moving van and the baby carriage (Genesis

12–22); a lad who felled a giant with smooth stones (1 Samuel 17), only to be felled later by a prophet's rebuke of his adulterous and murderous royal over-reach (2 Samuel 11–12); a poor teenage girl who said yes to an angel's offer of a turbulent future with a controversial son (Luke 1); fishermen and tax gatherers and prostitutes and revolutionaries who left their small everythings (Mark 1:16–20; Luke 19:1–11; John 4) to follow One who had already left his very large everything to find them (John 1; Philippians 2; Hebrews 1); a carpenter nailed to a crass wooden contraption (Matthew 27; Mark 15; Luke 23; John 19); and mournful women walking their solemn duty, who fall to their knees at a glimpse, through the morning haze, of a stone rolled away (Matthew 28; Mark 16; Luke 24; John 20). These surprising and compelling stories are our stories. The more we hear and tell them and even argue about them at the same table, the more God can bring us together as one very diverse but formed and transformed people.

After all, a liberal Dallas church and a conservative Houston church each found its way to a convicting, inspiring Bible passage that called them both, then to a mission that fit the passage—and in the mysterious ways of God, all this led them to one another. The more God forms us by these stories, read in each other's company, the more we'll learn to have our many disagreements "for the sake of heaven," and the more likely it is that we'll join in God's great mission to the world—a mission that transcends our differences and helps us, ultimately, to find one another.

NOTES

1. This is a United Church of Christ term for churches who welcome gay and lesbian men and women into full church membership and ordained ministry, and who perform gay and lesbian weddings. Other denominations use other terms for similar stances.

2. The quotation comes from Albert Mohler on the Southern Baptist Convention website. SBC resources on homosexuality can be found at http://tinyurl.com/ybn9nove.

3. In 2015, the Southern Baptist Convention took steps to end, or at least qualify, the policy of reparative therapy. Bruce Schreiner of the Associated Press covered this shift in his piece, "Reparative Therapy Criticized by Southern Baptist Theologian," *AP News*, October 5, 2015, http://tinyurl.com/y84yj62v. Opponents saw no essential change in the policy. E.g., Michael Fitzgerald, "Confusing Southern Baptist Statement Rejects 'Ex-

Gay' Therapy, Embraces 'Biblical Conversion Therapy,'"
Towleroad, October 6, 2015, http://tinyurl.com/ydf8txu8.

4. From a transcript of Aaron Sorkin, "The West Wing,"
Season 1, Episode 21: "Lies, Damn Lies, and Statistics,"
http://communicationsoffice.tripod.com/1-21.txt

5. In the 1970s, Harold Lindsell, who was at the time the
editor in chief of *Christianity Today*, wrote *The Battle for
the Bible* (Zondervan, 1978). In it, Lindsell chided
evangelicals whose definition of biblical authority he
deemed inadequate—which for him meant too low. Four
decades later, Mark Galli, *CT's* current editor, calls
Lindsell's book "divisive and unhelpful." Nonetheless,
he has called for another battle for the Bible, calling
Christians to remain faithful to the teachings of
scripture against the winds of culture and pseudo-
Christian revisions. "Why We Need the New Battle for
the Bible," *Christianity Today*, September 24, 2015,
http://tinyurl.com/ybgejefe.

6. The other three are Romans 1:26–28, 1 Corinthians 6:9–11,
and 1 Timothy 1:10. Some cite the Genesis account of
Sodom and Gomorrah in Genesis 18—19, which features
homosexual activity among its abuses.

7. This characterization does not hold true
universally—especially for evangelical pastors. For
example, see, Sara Pulliam Bailey, "Conservative
Evangelicals Join Letter Denouncing Trump's Order on

Refugees," *Washington Post*, February 8, 2017,
https://tinyurl.com/ycpwrc03. But a 2015 LifeWay
Research poll found that 86 percent of evangelicals want
more secure borders and 68 percent "say their church has
never encouraged them to reach out to immigrants."
John Blosser, "86 Percent of Evangelicals Want More
Secure Borders," *Newsmax*, March 13, 2015,
https://tinyurl.com/yco3w99e.

8. Abigail Geiger, "Five Facts on How Americans View the
Bible and Other Religious Texts," *FactTank* (Pew
Research Center blog), April 14, 2017, http://tinyurl.com/
y7pybnkg.

9. Mark Ambinder, "Fallwell Suggests Gays to Blame for
Attacks," ABC News Online, September 14, 2001,
http://tinyurl.com/yb4704d8.

10. Rachel Held Evans, "The Mainline and Me,"
RachelHeldEvans.com, April 3, 2012, http://tinyurl.com/
ycom7ww6.

11. "KAVANNAH (Intention)," B'nai Jeshurun, BJ.org,
http://tinyurl.com/y7erudtf.

7

CHRISTIAN MINGLE

We know that shared beliefs are the best foun-
dation for a lasting and fulfilling relationship.
                    —Christian Mingle home page[1]

Rev. Dr. Eric Elnes and his Scottsdale, Arizona,
UCC church hatched in 2005 a project called Crosswalk America, with the express mission to "bring
visibility to progressive Christianity." The chosen
means would be a long walk across a big country. He
summoned the willing, gathered suitable footwear,
screwed up their courage, and set out on their journey from Scottsdale to Washington, DC, armed
with confidence that, in an age dominated by a very
visible conservative Christian voice in culture, the

nation's ear should at least have a chance at a progressive Christian message.

This liberal lot would navigate a wide swath of conservative territory. Peruse an electoral map of the United States, and you'll spot nary a blue state between Scottsdale, Arizona, and Washington, DC. Sometimes Eric and his crew had to search hard for progressive faith communities who would host them along the way—their customary practice throughout the trip. In Eagar, Arizona, however, Eric decided to break custom and visit the most fundamentalist church he could find. He and his team scoured the local listings and landed Jesus First Baptist Church, which featured American flags prominently in the four corners of the ad and veritably screamed, "Conservative Christianity." Obviously, this would be the one.

First, they made arrangements. When the Crosswalk America group stepped into town on a Saturday, Eric phoned the church and asked to join them the next morning in worship. He shared with the pastor a bit about the mission of Crosswalk America and gave fair warning that his group customarily came with a camera crew to document their visit. Eric was predictably surprised when the Jesus First Baptist people said, "Sure, come on over."

The pastor's consent did not allay the group's

fears. Eric could recruit only one stalwart companion to cross the Left-Right border with him that fateful Sunday morning. The walkers' fear made sense. After all, JFBC seemed arrayed against everything these committed progressives stood for, and for everything they stood against. The Crosswalk team expected opposition, ridicule, or worse. Why poke the bear? Most stayed home. Eric and Leslie trudged through the streets of Eagar to church, not untroubled themselves.

When the two arrived at the church building, with their camera crew in tow, the pastor met them at the front door. Eric offered some literature, which the pastor carried with him to his office as he directed them to an adult ed class studying Revelation and the second coming of Jesus. Neither one could remember a class or a sermon on Revelation in their own kind of church, and the focus on Jesus's second coming felt strange to their progressive selves. That's what they'd expected. So far, so usual.

When worship began, though, things got weird. Early in the service, the pastor introduced the visiting Crosswalkers to his congregation as "these people who are walking across America for Jesus." Then he asked Eric to tell them about his mission. Almost shocked by the positive tone, Eric summoned the nerve to rise and say, "I'm Rev. Eric, and this is

Leslie, and we're walking this land because we want the nation to know that there is kind of Christianity where Jesus is our way to God, but we acknowledge other ways, too. . . . Where enduring and faithful love between two people is celebrated, whatever their gender," and so on, through the list of progressive beliefs called the Phoenix Affirmations.[2] There followed a dramatic and awkward silence. But surprisingly to Eric and Leslie, no vegetables were flung, and no curses uttered. Whew! Relief. Then, as the congregation sang their praise songs, the pastor asked them to join hands and surround Eric and Leslie, singing "Shine, Jesus, Shine!" He mentioned Crosswalk favorably several times in his sermon. And finally, as if all that weren't enough, as worship neared its close and the offering plates began to circulate through the pews, the pastor begged the congregation's permission to dedicate the entire offering to these progressive, different-than-them walkers. Afterward, the fundamentalists and the progressives chatted over potluck on the lawn.

"It's like this magic happened," Elnes said. "Rather than rejecting us the congregation ended up embracing us. They saw we were walking for Jesus and that's what mattered most to them. They didn't come around to our point of view but it was a magical moment that suggested to us that it's possible to find common ground, it's possible to listen to one another, it's possible to look into each other's eyes knowing you disagree strongly and find people's humanity. If we can do that, we have what it takes to work through these difficult issues."[3]

Surely this is the kind of thing Paul pictured when he told his Corinthian friends that there should be "no divisions among you" (1 Corinthians 1:10).

FIRST THINGS FIRST

During the Thirty Years War in Europe, Christians killed Christians in numbers that make the US Civil War look small. Amid the carnage, an obscure German pastor called Rupertus Meldenius wrote words that should be nailed to every church door and pulpit across our divided land. As one of the bloodiest feuds in the history of Christianity raged around him, as his own parishioners killed and died over doctrines, this humble pastor offered his plea for a ceasefire: "In essentials, unity; in non-essentials, liberty; and in all things, charity."[4]

Maybe our Jesus First Baptist Church pastor had read Meldenius. When a one-way-Jesus, the-Bible-condemns-homosexuality, Christianity-is-about-heaven-and-hell, Jesus-first Baptist pastor extravagantly welcomed a many-ways-to-God, God-blesses-homosexual-unions, Jesus-is-mainly-about-doing-justice UCC pastor, it was because the Baptist pastor ranked something above winning the culture wars: "I want to introduce you to two people who are walking across America for Jesus."

Eric Elnes once confided in me that, as a progressive Christian pastor, he could not have imagined handing over his congregation's ear to itinerant anti-abortion or anti-gay Christians. But here was a conservative shepherd standing smilingly by as a visitor regaled his conservative flock with challenges to, among other things, their theology (he normally preached one way to God through Jesus), their view of revelation (for this pastor, the Bible is the literal word of God), and their ethics (for his church, proper love and marriage are between a man and a woman).

What could explain such non-defensive, even affirming hospitality? It seems that in a moment of Christian authenticity, the Jesus First Baptist Church pastor actually did put Jesus first. The laundry list of his disputes with the Crosswalkers could have filled a six-month sermon series. But he chose to focus instead on what they had in common and recognize that, as different as their convictions might be, these Crosswalkers were "Jesus First" people, too.

Right and Left stayed in the same room because they ultimately managed to care more about an essential that brought them together than they did about the nonessentials that they'd been taught defined them. Jesus called his disciples to tell the world about him (Matthew 28:16–20; Acts 1:8), so a fundamentalist church applauded and blessed these progressive Christians who were walking American roads to do that, and they worshipped with them. The thrill of the story is that they all discovered, for a moment (and to their utter surprise), that they could do what Christians do together. Essentials outranked nonessentials.

THE ANGEL IS IN THE DETAILS

Naming our essentials and navigating the rest sounds simple. But Christians and churches have lately lengthened our unspoken "essentials" lists and defined ourselves by a plethora of nonnegotiables that divide us. Two of these adequately illustrate the problem: Do you believe in the virgin birth? Do you believe God blesses monogamous homosexual relationships? Ask those two questions across Christendom, and fights will break out. And they're only the very beginning. Define those two parts of Christian disagreement among your nonnegotiable essentials, and you can kiss the other half of Christ's church good-bye.[5]

Christians have defined people in or out of the club for, among other things, the way we baptize (e.g., Episcopalians sprinkle, Baptists immerse, Quakers do neither); what we believe about abortion (most progressives emphasize a woman's right to choose it, while most conservatives believe it violates Moses's "thou shall not kill"); whether we believe God wants us to use musical instruments in worship or not (one branch of the Campbellite Church of Christ embraces instruments, another eschews their use); whether we believe Jesus and God are of one substance (Greek: *homo-ousios*) or of like substance (Greek: *homoi-ousios*); whether or not we believe military involvement is a valid undertaking for Christians; whether we believe that God will send some people to hell in the end and for what they'll be sent there; whether we believe Jesus is coming back soon or not, and whether there will be a thousand-year tribulation before or after that event; whether speaking in tongues is a necessary marker for salvation; whether Christians ought to risk being arrested for civil disobedience or not; and on and on. All of these definitions and more could have threatened to break up that unified Eagar, Arizona, worship across difference that so inspired us. Praise God, they did not.

At Yale Divinity School in 2010, Dr. Wesley Avram and I taught a summer course called "The Big-Tent Church." For one intensive week, we and the pastors and leaders in our course read and reflected on what it would take to host wide Christian difference peaceably and constructively in the same congregation. As we began to plan for that course, one of the first questions Wes and I asked was, "What are my nonnegotiables?" We did a facetious sort of "Rocks, Paper, Scissors, Shoot" drill and were surprised that we both blurted "the divinity of Christ." Even with that shared starting point, though, we found the task of identifying our actual Christian essentials difficult, and our students had an even more difficult time. Try it yourself, and you'll see. But without this conscious process, Christians run the risk of operating in unconsidered default modes. This book won't define essential Christianity, but I do hope to prompt the conversation.

American churches in our time spend more time crafting vision statements than doing the hard and faithful work of intentionally and prayerfully defining what makes someone Christian. That's partly because it's a high-degree-of-difficulty dive. It risks defining some people in and others out, which prompts an allergic reaction from many progressives. And it risks allowing that any part of the Bible is not as important as the rest, which some conservatives, who claim the Bible as their only creed, won't allow. But if we don't intentionally work out those definitions, we risk operating on unconsidered assumptions.

An example: a church community who believe that "inclusion" is a Christian essential, may extravagantly welcome gay, lesbian, and transgendered persons but harshly marginalize anyone who does *not* believe that God blesses homosexual unions or transgender identity. The website will not pronounce, "We believe that anyone who opposes homosexual activity or transgender identity is going to hell" or "We believe that all *true* Christians and churches include gay and lesbian men and women fully in their lives, ministry, and membership." But anyone who tries to join that church or serve on a board or teach Sunday school or guest-speak and makes her or his reservations about homosexuality known will often be quickly marginalized or refused, or will discover otherwise that she or he is not numbered among the blessed. When progressive churches include, they tend not to include the non-includer—whether by subtle or direct means.

Here's a project. The next time you attend your

own church, become a theological anthropologist for an hour. Put on an outsider's eyes, and sleuth out the unstated essentials of your community. You'll surely gather some data from the song choices, litanies and other liturgy, prayers, the selected Bible verses, and sermons; you'll also learn from less considered, and therefore maybe more revelatory, things like the seating order, the ethnic and political makeup of the congregation, the kind of people who are most enthusiastically greeted, the style of worship, the kinds of events or activities announced, and the way people talk about Christians or churches or just other people who are not in the room. Track who is the butt of the preacher's theological or political joke, who is included in the "we" that the preacher and other speakers assume, and who is excluded from that "we."

These coded messages amount to the haphazard way many churches communicate our haphazardly defined essentials. When you've finished your anthropological hour, record your results and take them to your staff (if you're a pastor) or your pastor and leaders (if you're not). Ask if your list correctly identifies their intended essentials.

A CHURCH ABOUT TOWN

On his office door at Duke Divinity School, the renowned theologian Stanley Hauerwas used to display a Mennonite poster that read, "A modest proposal for peace: let the Christians of the world resolve not to kill each other." When students complained that this was "just another example of Christian self-centeredness," he always replied, "I agree that it would certainly be a good thing for Christians to stop killing anyone, but you have to start somewhere."[6]

This Hauerwas anecdote came to mind when I read Jon Stewart's postmortem of the 2016 presidential election. In a strong response to the way post-election bitterness played out, the long-time host of Comedy Central's *Daily Show* named the hypocrisy with these words: "There's now this idea that anyone who voted for [Trump] has to be defined by the worst of his rhetoric. . . . In the liberal community, you hate the idea of creating people as a monolith. 'Don't look at Muslims like a monolith. They are individuals, and it would be ignorant.' But everybody who voted for Trump is a monolith—is a racist. That hypocrisy is . . . real in our country."[7] As with Americans from the progressive versus the Trump camp, so with Christians from different kinds of churches: when we don't meet one another, we remain ignorant of one another and make assumptions that hurt everyone involved.

A progressive Christian example of this stereotyping reached me through a Facebook string. A couple days after the election, a frustrated friend of mine posted a good question: "Huh, 81% of Evangelical Christians liked a man with 3 wives & no history of charitable giving. Why?" Many, many non-Evangelicals had the same question. The incongruity of that 81 percent statistic in the context of long-held Evangelical values of marital fidelity, clean speech, and other moral convictions even caused more than a few prominent Evangelical leaders to ask versions of this question. My friend's question was valid, but the long string of progressive responses to her post revealed both tribal venom and willful ignorance. Here's a sample:

- "Because for Evangelical Christians it's 100% faith and 0% works."
- "Because they like authoritarians."
- "One is the cheap-and-easy 'abortion issue.' Evangelicals like that one because it makes them feel virtuous and holy to oppose abortion, without actually helping women or babies."

- "The other is that Evangelicals think women should not have power, ever, over men."
- "Evangelicals love a reality TV star like nothing else, there are many mansions, and fortunes out there that were bought and paid for from televangelists' received 'donations.'"
- "Because no vagina."

The replies continued relentlessly. The first accuses evangelicals of built-in hypocrisy, the third can only imagine that anti-abortion activists act out of a desire to feel superior, the fifth pictures Evangelicals as white-trash reality-TV addicts, and the second, fourth, and sixth picture evangelicalism as insistently anti-female. As a friend of many justice-doing, humble, *Game of Thrones*–watching, women-honoring Evangelicals, I found the string painfully inaccurate.

As much as the anti-Evangelical slurs in my friend's string bothered me, the "they" language spoken by Christians about other Christians hurt more. The people in this blue Christian tribe had very obviously never met the people in that red Christian tribe, and they surely didn't consider them family. One of the frustrated lefties even posted as much:

"I know only progressive Christians." This klatch gathered in the safety of their own string and hurled generalizations across the divide. They didn't know any one Evangelical but remained smugly certain that they knew "Evangelicals."

To solve American polarization, simply knowing one another personally would be a great first step. When the Republicans captured a majority in the House of Representatives in 1994, two years into Bill Clinton's presidency, their leader, Newt Gingrich, made a fateful decision: he urged the Republican representatives to move their families back to their home districts instead of living in Washington. That doesn't initially sound ominous. In fact, it makes some sense for a representative to live among the people he or she represents. But here's the rub: previously, Democratic and Republican legislators, because they all lived in town, had attended events together or socialized in each other's homes on weekends. They'd watched each other's kids play Saturday soccer or act in Friday-night school plays. That tradition of shared off-the-battlefield experiences began to erode in 1994, which happens to mark the start of the rapid increase in political polarization in the United States. No longer acquainted away from the debate floor, the legislators no longer had a known face to match with the ideas they opposed. In the absence of that social bond, bipartisanship gradually disappeared.[8]

Christians are called to be a family about town, baptized into a clan with "neither Jew nor Greek, slave nor free, male and female"—all one in Christ Jesus (Galatians 3:28). This family identity has strong implications for the way we're called to keep community. The apostle Paul once chastised his Corinthian congregation members for suing one another in Roman courts. His language offers an alternative to our current habit of talking *about* one another, instead of to one another: "When one of you has a grievance against another, does [she or] he dare go to law before the unrighteous instead of the saints? . . . To have lawsuits at all with one another is already a defeat for you. Why not rather suffer wrong? Why not rather be defrauded? But you yourselves wrong and defraud—even your own brothers [and sisters]!" (1 Corinthians 6:1, 7–8 ESV).[9]

FINDING ONE ANOTHER

Christians should settle our differences—or at least air them to one another—around the family dinner table. That's Paul's point. Our chances of living out Jesus's prayer "that they all may be one" would skyrocket if we actually knew one another. Yet we haven't even met a lot of our brothers and sisters. In fact, we've been avoiding them. Here's the rub with that avoidance strategy: statistics and arguments rarely unseat prejudice. We change our minds about a group when we experience actual people from it, in all their stereotype-defying complexity. Significant transformations or openings of mind usually happen through experience rather than argument.

To research his hilarious, profound book *The Year of Living Biblically*, A. J. Jacobs immersed himself fully in biblical literalism. He interviewed people who look at the Bible that way, including the Amish, the founder of the Creation Museum in Kentucky, a member of the Jehovah's Witnesses, the fundamentalist pastor of Jerry Falwell's church, and others he frankly could not fathom. Those interviews surely gave Jacobs, an agnostic, plenty of ammunition for ridicule, yet the book's tone is respectful. He found a way to access compassion for the people who live day-to-day the literalism he might have set out to mock. Even his critique of hyper-literal fundamentalism (it is not actually literalist, but selectively literalist) has a relational depth that it wouldn't have had without direct conversation. Experience of people who frequent these odd worlds tempered his treatment of them, because they became real people.

Experience of our opposite's world will do that for us, too.[10]

You and I don't have to spend a year living as our opposites to break down our stereotypes. And some of us can't picture ourselves cold-calling a political opposite and saying, "Let's have breakfast." We may need baby steps before we leap. A less extreme entrée to Christian Mingle is simply reading what our opposite reads or hearing what she hears. So set your news feed differently. If you're a *Newsweek* reader, subscribe to the *Weekly Standard* or *National Review* also. If you usually do Fox News, watch MSNBC for a while, too. Subscribe to both *Christianity Today* and *Christian Century*. Find a blogger from the other side of the church aisle and the political aisle. Create your own news algorithm that demands difference

As we read perspectives that aren't ours, this other-understanding purpose will dictate a way of hearing and reading that may be new to us. We're out to learn and build compassion, not to condemn. That means when we arrive at those pages or podcasts, we don't scour them for worst-case fodder ("Can you believe they said that?!") and post it on Facebook for our tribe to deride them along with us. Make it your project to understand the content from the inside. That means offering the benefit of the doubt. Ask what needs the author or speaker meets by this way of being American or Christian. Find common ground with the desires that attract people to this view of the world. If you can't find a friend to talk to, mingle with the worldview in print or on screen.

Making a friend is even better. Go on a field trip: worship at a church whose beliefs you can't understand, and then hang out. Meet the people who attend. Make your way to a coffee line or water cooler conversation with a partisan whose politics you don't understand, and strike up relationship. If we step into these risky places, we'll experience what Francis of Assisi prayed: "O divine Master, grant that I may not so much seek . . . to be understood as to understand."

My childhood years in the small, white, working-class village of Sheridan, Oregon, featured a whole lot of white, working-class sameness. But every year, a welcome outsider interrupted that homogeneity through our high school's foreign-exchange program. We hosted students from exotic places, including Kiko from El Salvador, Nina from England, Monica from Chile, Dow and Blackie from South Africa, Cecilia from Mexico, and Scott from Ohio.

I've wondered in our time if an urban, progressive,

African American church in Chicago might send exchange students to a rural, white, conservative church in Wyoming, and vice versa. Or if just those two youth groups could collaborate in mission somewhere, a la Cathedral of Hope and its Southern Baptist partners. Or maybe we could build the trust to send our kids from progressive to conservative and from conservative to progressive churches across town for more than a stare-through-the-glass Sunday. If experience transforms, let's get intentional about multiplying experiences. Or better yet, let's meet one another when we're all out of our comfort zone. We should venture out on study trips to faraway Bible lands like Greece or Rome or the Holy Land with pilgrims intentionally gathered from Left, Right, and middle.

If Christians want to stop shooting at one another from a distance—to take Stanley Hauerwas' advice and stop killing one another—then red and blue Christians need to know each other. We can get as creative as we want about how, and we all ought to do just that. But for starters, it could be as simple as a rainbow church and a Southern Baptist church collaborating in mission—this time more intentionally than our featured churches did it. It could look like Crosswalkers and Jesus First worshippers singing "Shine, Jesus, Shine" together at the top of their lungs. I have no doubt that the Christians who built blue schoolhouses and watched kids learn there or felt the "magic" of that Sunday morning in Eagar, Arizona, began to talk about "those lefties" or "those fundies" differently than they had before.

Our ancient North African brother Tertullian must have had this in mind when he reported how Christians had lain down their lives for one another and said: "See how they love one another!"[11]

NOTES

1. I here use the name of a popular Christian dating and matchmaking website, Christian Mingle (www.christianmingle.com), to characterize a better way of being church.

2. Eric Elnes, *The Phoenix Affirmations: A New Vision for the Future of Christianity* (San Francisco: Jossey-Bass, 2006).

3. Eric Elnes tells the story of this magical encounter in chapter 4 of *Asphalt Jesus: Finding a New Christian Faith along the Highways of America* (San Francisco: Jossey-Bass, 2007).

4. The maxim in Latin is *In necessariis unitatem, in non-necessariis libertatem, in utrisque charitatem.* It has often been falsely attributed to the fourth-and-fifth-century

luminary Saint Augustine, but it actually originated with our much more obscure pastor Rupurtus Meldenius in the midst of perhaps the bloodiest Christian feud in history, twelve centuries later. For another view on the quotation's origin, see Dr. Steve Perisho's comment in James J. O'Donnell, "A Common Question from 'Augustine'?," Georgetown University, http://tinyurl.com/y9se9kh6.

5. The essential that pops up again here is the one we noted in the last chapter: the question of how we read scripture. How we look at the virgin birth and the passages that condemn (a kind of) homosexual activity lies behind the specific debate about the belief claims.

6. *Unleashing the Scripture: Freeing the Bible from Captivity to America* (Nashville: Abingdon, 1993), 63.

7. Laura Bradley, "Jon Stewart Points Out Liberal Hypocrisy in the Wake of Donald Trump's Win," *Vanity Fair*, November 17, 2016, http://tinyurl.com/yb8uboqp.

8. For more, see Tom Davis, Martin Frost, and Richard Cohen, *The Partisan Divide: Crisis in Congress* (Campbell, CA: Premiere, 2014); and Johanna Neuman, "Gingrich and the Roots of Political Polarization," *Los Angeles Times*, September 22, 2009, http://tinyurl.com/y7bbsmwo.

9. I've chosen the English Standard Version because, in the interest of gender inclusion, the New Revised Standard Version has jettisoned the accurate translation of the

Greek word *adelphoi*, which describes the church as a family of brothers and sisters (the NRSV renders it "believers" instead). Paul's exhortation relies on the spectacle of a family going to court against itself.

10. A.J. Jacobs, *The Year of Living Biblically: One Man's Humble Quest to Follow the Bible as Literally as Possible* (New York: Simon & Schuster, 2007).

11. Tertullian, *Apology* 39.7, quoted from Tertullian, *Apology, De Spectaculis*, Minucius Felix, *Octavius*, Loeb Cassical Library Volume 250 (Cambridge, MA: Harvard University Press, 1931).

8

COURAGEOUS CONVERSATIONS

All grant that unity is good, but not all agree
that it is pleasant.

—Saint Augustine (*City of God* 63:5)

The Broadway musical *Hamilton* swept through 2016
in the United States like a hurricane. It won eleven
Tony Awards, a Grammy, and an Oscar nomination,
and sold out astronomically priced seats nightly at
the Richard Rodgers Theatre. More importantly,
Hamilton transformed the picture of our nation-
founding generation for millions of Americans. Lin-
Manuel Miranda tells the story of the first US Trea-
sury Secretary, Alexander Hamilton, in a hip-hop
cadence, the perfect idiom for the smackdown
Hamilton-Jefferson cabinet battles and red-hot

polemic between all the players who built the American democracy.

In tribute to the play, hip-hop artists Tariq Trotter and Ahmir Thompson wrote a belated, brief prologue called "No John Trumbull."[1] In it, they remember with us Trumbull's classic painting of the Founding Fathers waiting patiently in line to sign the Declaration of Independence, "looking all humble" and "with not one grumble." But our artists know the polemic that peeled the paint off those eighteenth-century walls when the founders argued a point—the red-in-the-face frustration of long hours in conference. "The reality is messier and richer, kids. The reality is not a pretty picture, kids." Then they widen to the president and his staff: "Every cabinet meeting is like a full-on rumble." Before the curtains go up, they issue one last fair warning: "What you are about to see is no John Trumbull."

These vicious battles between Hamilton and Jefferson and (offstage) Adams alarm folks who have imbibed the romantic image of harmony among the founders. But Miranda, Trotter, and Thompson flag an insight we've all but forgotten in our polarized times: it's good that we have each other. For all their mutual savagery, these opposites tapped even more genius together than any one of them could have managed separately. Five Thomas Jeffersons would not have done it. Slavery would have lasted longer, or the states would have divided into one southern nation and one northern one long before Lincoln's time, or we might not have gotten one federal government at all. Hamilton belonged to the New York Manumission Society, and a five-Hamilton cabinet would likely have moved earlier on slavery. But, given his elitist tendencies and his distrust of democratic elections, the Hamiltonian United States might have become an independent western annex of British monarchy. If that cabinet room had featured one founder with five "Amen!" voices, the US democracy would not have survived the eighteenth century, But these five in the same room hatched the American Experiment—a battle of contending voices and checks and balances that produced something far more brilliant and enduring than any one of them could have come to on his own. In spite of their ruthless polemic, they stayed close enough to build something larger.

THE HARD PATH TO TRUTH

It may surprise you that I approve of the founders' scrimmages. Having read this far, you may imagine that I seek harmony at all costs. Maybe you've even begun to think I don't care about beliefs, convictions, truth, and justice—that I favor some sort of bland Christian congeniality.

Au contraire! I love truth, actually. In fact, I care so much about keeping difference together precisely because I think we have a better shot at truth together than we have if we keep ourselves separate from one another. "Iron sharpens iron," scripture says (Proverbs 27:17), and Left and Right sharpen one another. US Supreme Court justice Oliver Wendall Holmes drives the concept home in his 1919 argument for the constitutionality of free speech. In his dissenting opinion for Abrams vs U.S., Holmes writes,

> When men have realized that time has upset many fighting faiths, they may come to believe . . . that the ultimate good desired is better reached by free trade in ideas—that the best test of truth is the power of the thought to get itself accepted in the competition of the market, and that truth is the only ground upon which their wishes safely can be carried out.[2]

In our age, when politicians tailor-make their audiences to avoid opposition and university students shout down speakers whose words make them feel

"unsafe," Holmes's words shout the value of conflicting ideas, boldly stated, and I shout my loud
"Amen!"

In fact, my only problem with our splendid Little
Blue Schools project and our progressive-welcom-
ing Jesus First Baptist worship service is the short
shelf lives of their relationships. A mission project
gets done, and a worship service goes well. These
moments inspire us, but they don't last and the story
doesn't continue, because these Christian brothers
and sisters of Texas and Arizona don't meet up the
next week and let their differences do their proper
work. They get high marks for good priority setting
in the moment, but they aren't on screen together
long enough to reap the full benefits of coming
together across their differences. The brass ring of
full cross-Christian benefits takes time to reach.

Pressed to boil the driving passion behind this
book down to a simple sentence, I'd write this: *God
gives us our difference as a gift—an asset, rather than a
threat.* I believe God gave the American church and
the whole republic both liberals and conservatives,
and that by our elective segregation we ungratefully
leave that gift unopened. Difference should come
together, not as a compulsory exercise to prove how
inclusive we can be, but because we gain insight and
strength from one another's diverse experiences and

perspectives. We should come together across difference because being different together makes us better. And reaping the full benefits of being "different together" takes time.

AN ANCIENT JOHN TRUMBULL

The earliest Christians sometimes looked like Madison, Jefferson, Hamilton, and Adams hammering it out. In a Jerusalem living room around 40 CE, a sort of "cabinet battle" among them broke out about Gentile inclusion. In Jesus, James, and Paul's time, male proselytes to Judaism were required to take on the ritual of circumcision to signal their full entry into Israel's covenant with God. This did not trouble the exclusively Jewish First Christian Church of Jerusalem. They kept kosher, probably kept Sabbath, and circumcised their kids, just as their scripture and their parents told them to. But when persecution scattered them into less Jewish lands, their message captivated Gentiles, too. Abraham's covenant and Moses's law dictated circumcising male converts, but Paul and Barnabas reported a strange dilemma: God's Spirit jumped into these newly Jesus-loving Gentiles before the apostles could even find a mohel. What to do?

Here's where our storyteller takes over. The

author of Luke and Acts was an early Christian John Trumbull. By this I mean that, like the famous painter of the American founders, Luke normally emphasizes the harmony and unity of the earliest church, sometimes at the expense of utter historical accuracy. He frequently removes the rough patches from the bits of Mark's Gospel that he includes in his own—like Jesus's anger and the anguished "My God, my God, why have you forsaken me?!" In Acts, he paints the earliest church as an ideal philosophical community, even making fishermen resemble the great Socrates himself.[3]

Acts 15 is no exception. That Jerusalem living room pits Paul and Barnabas, who challenge the tradition on the issue of circumcision (these are the liberals), against the (conservative) "circumcision party," black-letter Bible guys who know that the Hebrew Scriptures of their time don't even contemplate relaxing the requirement of circumcision. James, the main pillar of the Jerusalem church, presides over the conversation. Tempers could flare!

But John Trumbull (née Luke) paints it like this: Paul, Barnabas, and Peter recount stories of God's magnificent inclusion of Gentiles. The circumcision folks reply by citing the absence of precedents in Moses's Law, which requires circumcision and Torah observance. Then the sage elder James withdraws to chambers and returns with his historic compromise: "We should not trouble [with circumcision] those Gentiles who are turning to God, but we should write to them to abstain only from things polluted by idols and from fornication and from whatever has been strangled and from blood" (Acts 15:19–20 NIV). James decides the main issue in favor of the progressives (yes, Paul is a progressive in this picture!) but offers the conservatives symbols of Jewish cultural separateness (no meat sacrificed to idols, no sexual immorality, and no non-kosher foods). Accordingly, the group composes a joint letter, adjourns, and returns merrily to their newly unified ministries. The subjects of circumcision, meat offered to idols, sexual immorality, and kosher then promptly disappear from Acts, never appearing in that book's remaining thirteen chapters. Issue settled.

As the Roots would rap it, "The reality is messier and richer, kids."[4] The rest of the New Testament tells a much more complicated story. First, the conflict between Paul and the circumcision party was much more heated than Luke portrays it in Acts 15. In his vitriolic letter to the Galatians, Paul reports that "false brethren . . . were secretly brought in [to Jerusalem] (who came by stealth to spy out our liberty)" (Galatians 2:4). In fact, Galatians exists only because circumcision people—possibly sent out by James himself—have invaded this Gentile area code and claimed that Paul should have made circumcision compulsory. For his part, Paul calls down a curse on these interlopers, crassly suggesting that they re-circumcise themselves more thoroughly (Galatians 1:8–9; 5:12). He later calls messengers of this sort "dogs, evil-doers, the false circumcision" (Philippians 3:1). James himself even shows up elsewhere looking very different. His emissaries from the Jerusalem church to the one in Antioch pressure Peter to stop eating with Gentile Christians (Galatians 2:12).

As for the letter's stipulation about meat that has been sacrificed to idols, Paul treats it as an optional abstention (1 Corinthians 8–10), but John the Seer of the book of Revelation excoriates those who "entice the Israelites to sin so that they ate food sacrificed to idols and committed sexual immorality" (Revelation 3:12). That issue clearly kept brewing.

The Jerusalem council did not resolve these issues. The sides continued to oppose one another throughout the first century.[5] Even the genteel spirit maintained by all parties in the Acts 15 portrait seems a bit Trumbullesque. We probably should picture people frustrated with one another, red-faced with the passion of important debate. Paul and Barnabas and the circumcision party probably had to be separated a few times to avoid a row.

It is difficult to date and time the events of Acts 15, but the sheer number of references across the New Testament to conflict on the issue of circumcision tells us that vehement polemic abounded, both before and after James issued his decree. Luke clearly tried to capture the unity that did exist, and the fact of the gathering at least evinces some sort of joint identity among the earliest Chrisitan missionaries. But the illusion of original Christian unity and uniformity that the passage conveys may have cost us a bit, during the history of Christianity. It may have set us up to be surprised by our own strong disagreements, without a guide for how to resolve them, instead of prepared for the fact that high passion and strong conviction are good things that make for difficult conversations.

We contemporary American Christians can make our way back into the messy, rich room where conflict happens. Our Christian and American generation could become the one that turns the partisan battleships around toward one another and ushers our culture back to a robust, passionate, productive, high-stakes engagement across difference. We could become the people of Courageous Conversations.[6]

A HOUSE UNITED IN THE PEWS

Pastor Rich Nathan and the worshipers at Vineyard Columbus Church in Ohio don't all look alike. They don't all sound alike. In fact, those ten thousand faithful souls hail from 125 different nations around the world—125 nations!

Vineyard Columbus is Pentecostal in more ways than one. As a Vineyard Church, Pastor Nathan's crew is quite open to the movement of the Spirit through the charismatic gifts of tongues, prophecy, and healing that Acts 2–5 narrate and Paul enumerates in his list of spiritual gifts in 1 Corinthians 12. Staid mainline Christians might hear and see things they've never experienced before.

That would be healthy and good! But there is another way that Vineyard Columbus mirrors Pentecost. In Acts 2, God invites all kinds of nations, tribes, and peoples and languages to the grand opening of Jesus 2.0: the church. Peter preaches his famous Pentecost sermon to "Parthians, Medes, Elamites, and residents of Mesopotamia, Judea and Cappadocia, Pontus and Asia, Phrygia and Pamphylia, Egypt and the parts of Libya belonging to Cyrene, and visitors from Rome, both Jews and proselytes, Cretans and Arabs" (Acts 2:9–11). The nations gathered on that ancient Sunday and became the First Church of Jerusalem, and the nations gather today at Vineyard Columbus.

Here's more: in the book of Revelation, a divine guide escorts the seer, John, through the cosmic present and future. In one exalted moment, a vision transports John to the very throne room of God, where he sees "a great multitude that no one could count, from every nation, from all tribes and peoples and languages, standing before the throne and before the Lamb" (Revelation 7:9–10). This lonely, exiled, Jewish-Christian prophet, fed up with the vast Roman imperial state, pictures a God who has followers in every land.

My point: on any normal Sunday morning, Vineyard Columbus looks like Pentecost and heaven. Not bad alignment! And let's make no mistake here. Building a multiethnic community is far from easy. When Laura Meckler observes the recent increase in multiracial churches—their percentage nearly doubled, from 7 percent of American churches in 1998 to 13 percent in 2012—she illustrates political and cultural tensions that sometimes drive pastors to steer a less political course in their messaging.[7]

Because of this high degree of difficulty, many who host the big-tent congregations steer clear of the political part of Christian life altogether in favor of a harmony that ignores differences. Rich Nathan does the opposite. He capitalizes on differences, rather than avoiding them. Nathan kicked off the turbulent fall season of 2016 with a sermon series entitled "Different Together," which probed an array of controversial political and religious issues. He preached this wildly diverse lot of Christians through four of our main dividers, asking, "Can Republican and Democrat/Rich and Poor/Old and Young/Black and White Live Together in Peace?"[8] Pastors do this sort of thing every once in a while, but the makeup of this congregation makes this series different: Rich preached the series with everyone in the room. Vineyard Columbus fills every Sunday with a politically, socioeconomically, generationally, and racially diverse throng, so each sermon is not asking "Can *they* live together?" about someone out there. It's asking the question about *us*—the people next to one another in the pews. Can *we* live together? Rich Nathan's answer is a resounding "Yes!"

In June of 2017, Adam Hamilton found himself on the platform with *New York Times* columnist David Brooks as a featured guest of the Aspen Ideas Festival. The topic? "Seeing Gray in a World of Black and White." The Aspen organizers decided they wanted to hear from a middle-American pastor for one simple reason: this man has a clue about how to host political difference in his pews. Rev. Hamilton is the founding pastor of the now-twenty-thousand-member Church of the Resurrection in Kansas City. He estimates that his Sunday morning congregation is around 60 percent conservative, 40 percent progressive. In polarized times, those numbers are hard to hold—particularly when the leaders decide to address issues that divide people, which the Church of the Resurrection leaders do.

Hamilton routinely preaches on the most divisive of American topics—gun control, immigration, healthcare, homosexuality, and the other usual suspects. But the way he preaches them is not at all usual. He has developed a preaching strategy that purposely represents the different voices in the pews. He brings the courageous conversation to the pulpit, so that the opposing voices in the room hear their own convictions as he sets up the topic. His 2001 sermon series that became the book *Confronting the Controversies* illustrates the method.[9] In those sermons, the preacher presents opposing viewpoints understandingly, so that two-thirds through any sermon, the congregation feels "heard" and the person in the pew does not yet know on what side he will land. When Hamilton does finally show his cards and share his own convictions, it is with a humility that shows that he wants the conversation to go on, rather than pronouncing from on high. The result: people stay, even when they disagree, and the conversation does continue.

At a time when Americans normally vote with their feet and leave churches that don't play their political tunes, The Vineyard Columbus, and The Church of the Resurrection keep the conversation going. They face the same rugged problems all churches face, and their way of living with the tension aren't perfect. But they've found ways to be church together across difference that build the body of Christ and let its variety work "for the common good" (1 Corinthians 12:7).

A HOUSE UNITED IN CONVERSATION

On November 7, 2012, Minnesotans voted on an amendment to their state constitution that read, "Only a union of one man and one woman shall be valid or recognized as a marriage in Minnesota."[10] The days leading up to November 7 were tense. The most polarizing issue of this generation in the United States divided churches, neighborhoods, and the state. The amendment was the talk of the town.

In preparation for that crucial day, Christian leaders across the state subtly and not-so-subtly "educated" their congregations on how to vote correctly on the issue. On the Right, pastors produced five Bible passages that call homosexual activity an abomination (Leviticus 18:22 and 20:13) or list it among Christian vices (Romans 1:26–27; 1 Corinthians 6:9–10; 1 Timothy 1:9–10). On the Left, pastors who took recourse to scripture produced those same passages but in order to deconstruct them—either as not describing the modern experience of monogamous gay unions, or as not fitting Jesus's ethic of love, or as simply outmoded two millennia later. The righties reminded their flocks that no passage in scripture approves gay love. The lefties drew a big, red circle around the utter absence of this issue from Jesus's teaching in the Gospels. Very significantly, the righty churches and lefty churches did not talk to one another.

Wayzata Community Church, a large United Church of Christ congregation in the western suburbs of Minneapolis, chose another path. Partly by the accident of demographics and partly by missional design, WCC is a "big-tent church," with plenty of lefties and righties side-by-side in the pews on a Sunday. Mostly over the years their unity had been preserved by not talking about divisive issues. But John Ross, the senior minister, and a team of clergy and lay leaders decided it was time to take the church's big-tentishness out for a spin.

John's invitation began with these words:

> In contemporary American culture, people who strongly disagree on important things normally talk about one another instead of with one another. . . . Wayzata Community Church can be light to that world and demonstrate 'a more excellent way.' . . . On Monday evening [October 29] at 7 PM we will gather as a church family and talk respectfully with one another. . . . The Marriage Amendment lands in the middle of our culture wars, stirring deep emotions and strongly-held positions. We will gather that night and talk about it anyway . . . as a church family . . . who are even more committed to one another than we are to our stand on the issue. . . . Please join us. Our family meeting won't be complete without you. Add your voice to the conversation, courageously from the heart.

Four hundred congregants took their pastor up on his invitation and gathered that Monday evening.

Because I served on the Wayzata Community Church clergy staff then, I had a front-row seat for that inaugural Courageous Conversation. John led off with a prayer, I briefly introduced the available biblical arguments for yes and for no, and then Anne Harbison, our lay convener, laid out ground rules that would guide respectful dialogue, asking us to *testify* rather than to *campaign*.

Our team didn't set out to persuade or to force people to arrive at an official congregational statement on the issue, but rather to help them listen to and learn from one another. Our musician, Paul Franzik, taught us to answer each speaker with a sung refrain, "Hear what the Spirit is saying to the church. Thanks be to God. Thanks be to God." When the microphones went live, hesitant participants strode haltingly, then purposefully forward. The conversation began.

It went well. The sung refrain kept us from the usual American political genre of barroom brawl and opened us to the more decisively Christian work of discerning an important matter. The few accusations and acts of disdain clanged against the flow of the general civility of the evening. Several speakers shared how their experience of gay and lesbian men and women had changed their view. Another voice expressed faithful concern that we were ignoring clear Bible teaching to fit a social trend of our time. One young adult testified that as a lesbian woman, she felt strangely safe in the room. On an issue so divided and decided, one woman confessed in tears that she did not yet know what God thought about the matter. Words that would normally produce enmity and walkouts somehow fit together in the puzzle of difference.

We made mistakes, to be sure. Our insistence on personal experience rather than argument tilted the balance of the conversation leftward. (Experience-based epiphanies don't usually run toward a yes on the amendment.) Consequently, our first ten speakers praised inclusion until two or three late entries spoke—more courageous than all, in that setting. Many more people in the room had reservations or even opposed gay marriage than spoke out, and a couple of those conservatives later confided that they had felt silenced.

We also could have prepped people better on the issue. Our balanced on-site introductions gave a bite-sized summary of the tradition around homosexuality in the Bible and church, but that intro could not possibly cover details that would help participants engage deeply the ideas involved. In later iterations of what we have come to call "CouCons," in other churches, I've built prep sheets available days in advance. This tool presents the purpose and practices of CouCons and then provides a history of the issue that represents both or all arguments at their best. This practice facilitates a higher-level exchange.

Perhaps most disappointingly, we queued no follow-up conversations, frustrating those many who afterward asked to continue in smaller groups. (Once again, the church shorts the introverts.) I've since developed a follow-up mechanism that affirms participants for their attendance and civil candor, and then invites them to a deeper-dive event.

Finally, that night and again in later CouCons, we've found that simply tolerating one another's differences isn't enough. That was a very good goal on that night. It was our first-ever try. But as time goes, that minimal goal of tolerance shortchanges the good these chats could accomplish. Drawn beyond mere understanding and civility, we've learned to capitalize on our differences—not through compromise, but rather through understanding the competing narratives that ground our opposition and then building a new way of thinking together that preserves the variety, but joins both sides in a new, shared story.[11] I've subsequently produced tools designed to help groups move up the scale of engagement, from tolerance to mutual respect, to mutual learning, and finally to constructive collaboration.

To steal from Oskar at the end of Spielberg's *Schindler's List*, "We could have done more!" that Monday evening in Wayzata. But it was a good start: we brought our differences to a conscious, expressed level and still loved one another afterward. In the charged theological and political climate around gay marriage in 2012, we accomplished something difficult and rare. And, lo and behold, talking explicitly about our differences did not break the church. The next Wednesday, Wayzata Community Church continued to study the Bible together, and the next Sunday, we worshipped together, as usual.

A House United across the Street

Courageous Conversations deepen when two very different churches build the trust to talk together. For years, Stu Kerns has led Zion Presbyterian Church (PCA) in Lincoln, Nebraska. The PCA (Presbyterian Church of America) is a conservative brand of Presbyterianism—the one that, with J. Gresham Machen's help, formed Westminster Theological Seminary in Philadelphia back in the 1920s. In 2017, the nation heard about the PCA when Princeton Seminary awarded Rev. Tim Keller with an award but absorbed backlash because his denomination does not ordain women or bless gay unions.[12] This congregation mostly fits within the red majority in Lincoln and Nebraska.

Then there's Jim Keck. He leads First Plymouth Congregational Church, UCC, in downtown Lincoln, which brings a consistent progressive voice in Lincoln. In fact, pastors at First Plymouth performed gay marriages long before the rest of the church and nation caught up with the issue, and gay couples frequent the pews. On a single chilly fall weekend in 2016, FPC leaders participated in both a service of remembrance for transgender victims of abuse and a demonstration at the state capitol on behalf of the Standing Rock Native American community, whose sacred burial grounds have been destroyed by a pipeline project. The four-thousand-member First Plymouth Church is a big blue spot on the red map of Nebraska.

Stu the red and Jim the blue could simply play their congregation's song. Their lives would be easier if they preached to the choir of their conservative (Stu) or progressive (Jim) congregations. But both like constructive engagement more than the easy win. Stu hosts a local radio show called *Friendly Fire*, which brings a range of viewpoints into conversation on significant and divisive issues. His show's web page states the purpose: to highlight "1) the different ways our faith interprets events (worldview), 2) the importance of kind and civil debate, and 3) the important role the faith-community plays in Lincoln."[13]

For his part, Jim preaches sermons littered with very Evangelical-sounding terms like *conversion* and *relationship with Jesus*, which open his progressive lot to a more complex identity. FPC has also hosted a good old-fashioned Christian revival, featuring Otis Moss III, the dynamic pastor of Trinity United, a Pentecostal African American church in Chicago. Revivals are the dream of passionate conservative Christians. To liberals, though, they're suspect—too emotional, too unruly, too closed-minded, too wildly evangelistic. Nonetheless, there Jim is, calling in a revivalist to teach his people a whole new step in their dance with God.

Stu and Jim are not supposed to get along. The very red Zion Presbyterian and the oh-so-blue First Plymouth Congregational aren't supposed to get along. But there are Stu and Jim, sharing the airwaves on *Friendly Fire*,[14] and sharing a podium every once in a while in one or the other of their two churches. They ask hard theological and political questions together. They make jokes about their differences. They engage respectfully across disagreement.

There aren't a whole lot of intentionally-gathered big-tent churches these days in the polarized United States. So Stu and Jim's template fits better the usual left- or right-leaning congregations that fill our land. That sort of strong identification as conservative or progressive makes it unlikely that the Zions of the world will host a lot of progressives, or the First Plymouths of the world a whole lot of conservatives in their buildings Sunday to Sunday. How can Christians from very different congregations "come together across difference for the common good"? For most churches, it will look a lot like the story of Stu Kerns–Zion Presbyterian Church and Jim Keck–First Plymouth Church finding their way to one another.

That is all good. Not every church can or should be a big-tent church. There were Pauline churches, and there were Jamesian churches. Like finding like—what sociologists call homophily—can produce very effective community building, mission, and worship. Good sociological studies acknowledge the health of communities that hold one story together. It can also work well when we get political. I can imagine the hosts of heaven applauding, both when a left-leaning church builds into its mission and calls on its government leaders to care for widows and orphans (James 1:27) and when a right-leaning church reminds those same leaders that people who can work ought to work if they want to eat (2 Thessalonians 3:10). The magic happens when the left-leaning and the right-leaning church continue to engage one another so each will understand that theirs is not the only way and that they gain from the insights of the other. That engagement leads to the sort of trust that could make their Courageous Conversations brilliant.

IMAGINING OUTCOMES

Consider what American Christianity would look like today if the Machens and Fosdicks of the previous century had held their noses and stayed together in the same seminaries and churches—like the churches we've just visited. Imagine if they had kept going to chapel and class and worship and Bible study together, even when their differences cut them deep. If we are to believe the research of business scholars, the experience of military units, and the testimony of the eight congregations we've featured in these last three chapters, the outcome would be better Christianity.

"None of us wants abortions to happen," reads the imagined summit declaration, "and none of us wants women oppressed. More traditional voices among us forefront the first of these convictions, the absolute value of each human being—even the unborn whom some of us would call people and others of us, people in prospect. We are grateful for this gift, because it reminds us of the sanctity of life. Our more progressive voices remind us of the absolute value and dignified autonomy of women, along with the way churches and wider cultures have often ignored that value and dignity through the ages. We're also grateful for this gift. We commit ourselves to praying for and building the future of unborn children and of women." No one leaves the summit that produces this declaration fully happy, but all voices have been heard, and we have written a new, shared story together.

This sort of Christian collaboration would have helped us. We would also have made our way through a boatload of other conflicts, including gay marriage, very differently, if we had forced ourselves to sit across the pew and table from one another, rather than across the aisle or the Twittersphere. We could help one another, if we talked. And we could help our divided world.

NOTES

1. Tariq Trotter and Ahmir Thompson, *The Hamilton Mixtape*, "No John Trumbull," copyright 2016, Hamilton Uptown Limited Liability Company under exclusive license to Atlantic Recording Corporation.

2. Quoted in Andrew Cohen's, "The Most Powerful Dissent in American History," *The Atlantic* August 10, 2013, http://tinyurl.com/ybor9ugz.

3. See H. J. Cadbury, *The Making of Luke-Acts* (London: SPCK, 1936) and Abraham Malherbe, "'Not in a Corner': Early Christian Apologetic in Acts 26:26," in *Paul and the Popular Philosophers* (Minneapolis: Fortress Press, 1989), 147–50.

4. Trotter and Thompson, *The Hamilton Mixtape*, "No John Trumbull."

5. Paul's letters chronicle Gentile Christianity across the Mediterranean in the 50s CE. The book of Acts records the church's life from post-30 to around 60 CE, with an overlay of the concerns from the last decade. New Testament scholars are near consensus that Revelation represents Christianity in western Turkey in the last quarter of the first century, under the emperors Vespasian and/or Domitian. For a summary, with dissent, see Delbert Burkett's *An Introduction to the New*

Testament and the Origins of Christianity (Cambridge: Cambridge University Press, 2000).

6. The gold standard of guides on how to manage hard chats is Douglas Stone, Bruce Patton, Sheila Heen, and Roger Fisher, *Difficult Conversations: How to Discuss What Matters Most* (New York: Penguin, 1999). The book is grounded in Harvard-based research and applies to corporate, personal, civil, and religious settings.

7. Laura Meckler, "How Churches Are Slowly Becoming Less Segregated," *Wall Street Journal*, October 13, 2014, http://tinyurl.com/yc974ze7.

8. Vineyard Columbus, "Different Together," http://tiny url.com/y8j8lf2u.

9. Adam Hamilton, *Confronting the Controversies: Biblical Perspectives on Tough Issues* (Nashville: Abingdon, 2001). See also the very helpful *Leader's Guide* (Nashville: Abingdon, 2005).

10. "Minnesota Same-Sex Marriage Amendment, Amendment 1 (2012)," *Ballotpedia*, http://tinyurl.com/ y7s6e5cv.

11. David Anderson Hooker, a professor in Notre Dame's Kroc Institute for International Peace Studies, brilliantly crafts reconciliation and peacemaking strategies that involve this very narrative-based approach. He describes it in "CSUatMQ Interview with David Anderson

Hooker: Narratives and Reconciliation," interview by Liam Miller of Christian Students Uniting at Macquarie University (CSUatMQ), video, 27:14, uploaded by user Liam Miller, March 16, 2017, http://tinyurl.com/yc79orwo.

12. For one summary of the incident, see Celeste Kennel-Shank, "Princeton Seminary Cancels Award to Tim Keller, but Not His Lecture," *Christian Century*, April 4, 2017, https://tinyurl.com/ybzhsbsm.

13. "Friendly Fire," KLIN News Talk, http://www.klin.com/friendly-fire/.

14. One of two Kerns-Keck conversations on *Friendly Fire* is Stu Kerns, "Friendly Fire 9/24—Pastor Jim Keck," SoundCloud, September 24, 2016, http://tinyurl.com/yc2nzczz.

9

MISSION 4.0: HOW THE CHURCH CAN SAVE THE WORLD

Never doubt that a small group of thoughtful, committed citizens can change the world; indeed, it's the only thing that ever has.

—Margaret Mead[1]

In August 2017, Hurricane Harvey demolished the coastline of southeast Texas, bringing with it ferocious winds and record levels of rain and flooding. The heaviest rainfall in the recorded history of the

United States drove from their homes thousands and thousands of residents of Corpus Christi, Houston, Port Arthur, Katy, and a host of other cities and towns. Floodwaters claimed dozens of lives and many, many more livelihoods. Experts estimated the material damages in the hundreds of billions of dollars.

As floodwaters rose and then remained, Christians from Texas and all around the nation instinctively dropped what they were doing and dove in. They brought with them fresh water and daily necessities. They helped people escape danger and transported people to the safety of shelters and temporary housing solutions. They watched kids while parents absorbed the devastating damage and asked what was next. Christians from around the nation flocked to the danger zone and helped, because that's what faithful Christians do.

Living three hours away in Austin, Texas, and watching these heroic Christians rush in, I was struck by the composite body of Christ that showed up. The rescuers came from black churches and white churches, urban and rural churches, young and old churches, Pentecostal and staid churches, contemporary-music and traditional-music churches, Left and Right churches. Fundamentalists, liberals, and everyone in between laid aside differences, grabbed a bucket or a mop or a pack of water bottles and jumped in. One Houston resident noticed, "For a moment, all people work together and forget their political, religious, and economic differences. Believers from across denominations work shoulder to shoulder to provide rescue and relief."[2] No one even hesitated to worry about their political differences. Instinct carried Christians into the tragedy together to help. It was inspiring!

Christians came together for Hurricane Harvey because our world needed us. The urgency was palpable. What we miss during normal business hours is that our world needs us urgently these days, even when hurricanes don't rage. Our world needs us to bring relief amid the damaging sociopolitical storm we call polarization. Realizing this strange, simple truth ushers us toward Jesus' peculiar purpose for Christian unity across difference.

GOD'S PURPOSE FOR UNITY

As he tries to put words on the splendid sensation of unified worship, the ancient psalmist turns to pictures:

How very good and pleasant it is
>   when kindred live together in unity!
It is like the precious oil on the head,
>   running down upon the beard,
>   on the beard of Aaron,
>   running down over the collar of his robes.
It is like the dew of Hermon,
>   which falls on the mountains of Zion.
For there the LORD ordained his blessing,
>   life forevermore. (Psalm 133)

These are brilliant, sense-full, compelling images. And those who have experienced the glories of community can almost feel the oil flowing down. Christians across the spectrum building houses together is a beautiful and very oily Psalm 133 kind of thing. Left and Right singing "Shine, Jesus, Shine!" together inspires us and summons the splendid sensation of that oil flowing down Aaron's beard. When faithful folks who believe differently bring diverse perspectives into civil and constructive conversation, our community and our ideas get better, we can practically feel the fresh dew of Hermon sprinkling Zion. All of this is patently true. We Christians will thrive more and more as we learn to collaborate and build community across our differences, and it will be a rech experience.

But here's the world-widening truth of the gospel: as true as our psalmist's delicious words are, and as much as we may love the feeling of full community, in Jesus's vision, our unity is not ultimately about us. If all our hard work learning to come together across difference merely made Christians' lives more pleasant, I'm sure it would warrant a book. In fact, many write books today about how to be a happier, healthier church. But that's not why I've written this one. I do believe that Jesus came so that we "might have life and have it abundantly" (John 10:10), and as a citizen of the first century, he likely meant that communally. But I agree with Dietrich Bonhoeffer's challenging words: "Jesus Christ is 'the Man for Others'; therefore, the church is the church only when it exists for others."[3]

Don't get me wrong: I want the church to enjoy our rich new community across difference; but even more than that I want us to change the world for which Jesus died! When he utters the "new commandment . . . that you love one another as I have loved you" in John 13, Jesus doesn't take a breath before he tells its intended outcome: "all people will know that you are my disciples." When he prays "that they all may be one," he immediately also prays out unity's purpose: "so that the world will know that you [i.e., God] sent me." Jesus puts the dynamic succinctly in John 17:23: "I in them," he prays, "and you in me, that they may be perfected in unity, so that the world may know that you sent me and that you love them as you love me" (John 17:23 NASB). Oddly enough, the *telos*, the purpose, the end of Christian unity is not us. It's supposed to produce epiphanies about Jesus among people outside the church, in the world. When you and I and all our multi-perspectival crowd come together, those outside-the-church people learn something they didn't know before about the one who came to save them and us.

This revolutionary vision deserves a closer look. John 17:23 has three parts:

First, God inhabits Jesus's disciples. As he puts it, "I in them and thou in me." In John's Gospel, Jesus has already made the great equation, "I and the Father are one" (John 10:31). Here, Jesus prays that this whole divine presence will be "in" his disciples.

Second, that unified Godhead, Father and Son/ Creator and Redeemer, infuses itself into us and produces unity like the God-Jesus unity. Jesus names what happens when God-in-Jesus comes in: we become "perfected in unity" or "become wholly one." It is by this divine habitation—and not by even our best-intended, most tactically sound efforts to socially engineer unity—that Jesus's disciples become one. Christians who want unity ought to pray for revival.

Third, the world changes. Jesus pictures an outcome of all this unity-producing divine presence. He prays "that the world may know that you sent me and that you loved them as you loved me." When Christians love one another as Jesus loved us, as we become one, the world will notice and think new things about him.

When the God whose essential character it is to be one enters us, we become one as well. And when we become one, the world understands that God loves us and loves them.

EXEMPLARS OF UNITY

It's beautiful! And we find this powerful dynamic of divine indwelling producing divine-looking behavior all through the gospels. Jesus reveals that unified and unifying divine character by crossing all kinds of lines to bring people together on earth. Jesus crossed lines of race, religion, and politics impressively to bring difference together.

Despite the best efforts of preachers around the world, you and I really don't hear the sting twenty centuries later in the phrase "good Samaritan." But Jesus's first-century Jewish audience surely would have. The Samaritans were ethnically and religiously other—the hated rival. Talmud asks, "Why are the Samaritans excluded?" Rabbis then answer variously. First is religious impurity: "because they were mixed up with priests of the high places" (fostering idolatry) and because they worshipped in the wrong place (Mount Gerazim instead of Jerusalem—*The Babylonian Talmud*, Kuthim 2.7). Ethnically, it is "because they marry illegitimate women," which likely means "intermarriage with women of other races."[4] These religious and racial dividers produced enmity that simmered. These Jewish stereotypes of Samaritans sound as prejudiced and ill-informed as my progressive friend's Facebook string about evangelicals[5]—like rationalizations formed from a distance to affirm keeping distance. John's Gospel understates: "Jews have nothing to do with Samaritans" (4:9). Because of all this history and hatred, when Jesus praised a Samaritan (Luke 10), or sat down at a well with one (John 4), he was crossing charged boundaries of religious and ethnic exclusion.

Politically, consider the tension for Jews in first-century Palestine. Many Jews resented Roman rule for good reason. Pontius Pilate, who would come down through history for his role in Jesus's crucifixion, could be ruthless and once "mixed Jewish worshippers' blood with their sacrifices" in the Jerusalem temple (Luke 13:1). Most people vaguely and quietly complied, with occasional flare-ups, but Roman rule also produced two more extreme responses among the Jewish people: accommodation and rebellion. The priestly aristocracy in Jerusalem accommodated, because they gained power by serving Roman interests. Tax collectors also accommodated. These Jews signed on to fill Roman imperial coffers.

On the other extreme of the Jewish population in Jesus's time stood the Zealots. From the moment in 63 BCE when General Pompey led Roman forces to conquer Jerusalem, some Israelites advocated and occasionally fomented armed revolution. Then in 6 CE, Rome reformed the tax structure and asserted control by naming Palestine a province. These measures raised the temperature of the conflict and provoked the revolutionary spirit that gave birth to the "freedom fighters"—the Zealots. As Jesus began his ministry, then, tax collectors prospered by raising revenue for Rome, and Zealots plotted and schemed and lived to overthrow Rome. It would be hard to imagine two groups of Jews who hated one another more than the tax collectors and the Zealots.

Here's the brilliant moment: when it came time to hire his small and intimate twelve-person staff, Jesus chose one of each. The applicant pool of potential disciples was thick. The gospel accounts tell how huge throngs of people followed Jesus (e.g., Mark 3:7–8; 4.1). But Jesus chose Matthew the tax collector and Simon the Zealot to be two of his twelve (Luke 6:12–15). It's like starting a new legislative team with Paul Ryan and Bernie Sanders, or Al Sharpton and the Grand Wizard of the KKK. Awkward!

Not enough is made of the sheer audacity of Jesus's choice of both Matthew the tax collector and Simon the Zealot and what it ought to mean for subsequent Christian community. Our contemporary pulpits ring out with romantic images of Jesus reaching across boundaries to the sick, the marginalized, and the outcasts. But—still living the legacy of the fundamentalist-liberal controversy and enmeshed in the red state–blue state civil war—these same preachers leave aside Jesus's very risky and relevant choice of religious and political opposites. I've never once heard a sermon picturing Matthew and Simon working through their differences by a late-night campfire with Jesus. But we should hear about it, because Jesus brought them together for a reason.

JESUS, PART *DEUX*

In their better moments, the Jesus people naturally followed Jesus's lead and channeled his Spirit. From early on, leaders of the Jerusalem church instinctively came together across difference for something larger than themselves. The way they replicated his habit of community, you'd almost think that Jesus was "in them" (John 17:23).

The first lines to cross were ethnic and geographical. When God kept the apostles waiting in that upper room so long before Pentecost, they must have been curious about this "Holy Spirit" that Jesus had promised—the one that would provide "power" so they could "be my witnesses in Jerusalem, Judaea, Samaria, and to the ends of the earth" (Acts 1:8). But the apostles and a roomful of others had to wait. They made short work of replacing Judas, and then they waited.

Their first boundary was an ethnic one. God held back the promised Spirit till Pentecost filled Jerusalem streets to overflowing with foreigners. The whoooooosh and the tongues of flames that we celebrate each spring finally blew through as Peter and the rest gazed out at "Parthians, Medes, Elamites, and residents of Mesopotamia, Judea and Cappadocia, Pontus and Asia, Phrygia and Pam-

phylia, Egypt and the parts of Libya belonging to
Cyrene, and visitors from Rome, both Jews and
proselytes, Cretans and Arabs" (Acts 2:9–11). By
God's design, the raw material of the earliest congregation in Jerusalem would be, in the words of wild-
eyed John on Patmos, from "a great multitude that
no one could count, from every nation, from all
tribes and peoples and languages" (Revelation 7:9).
God placed the delivery room of the church smack
in the middle of a United Nations meeting.

If ethnic difference speckled those earliest
Jerusalem meetings, their next challenge was crossing religious boundaries and they faced it after they
left town. Everyone in our United Nations–like
photo of Pentecost in Jerusalem was religiously Jewish. When persecutions pushed these first Christians out into the wider world, though, a next difference threatened to divide the young church: what to
do with Gentiles. We thought Samaritans had a bad
name with Jews. Gentiles were worse. Jews called
them dogs. The first and second commandments of
Moses insisted on monotheism, but Gentiles honored countless gods, and Jews saw the polytheism
producing loose sexual morality. From a Jewish perspective, centuries of polytheism had stained Gentiles. Yet God had the audacity to call the young
church to host both Jews and Gentiles and then

charged them with authoring the conditions of that truce.

Despite their deeply ingrained biases, these Jesus people soon pushed through that boundary, too. Peter dreamed that God offered him a sheet full of non-kosher meats and insisted that he eat (Acts 10:1–33). Peter, Paul, and Barnabas watched Gentile after Gentile powerfully receive God's Spirit (Acts 15:7–12). In time, Paul, the former Hebrew of Hebrews, pictured God breaking down the dividing wall of hostility between Jews and Gentiles through Jesus's cross (Ephesians 2:11–22).

The mix also crossed class lines. This shows up early in Acts, where that first group in Jerusalem famously collects everyone's things and distributes them "as any had need" (Acts 2:44–45). It appears more subtly in Romans 16, where Paul greets a laundry list of Christians, whose names tell an important story. Bible sleuths have discovered that, like DNA at a modern crime scene, ancient names help us trace identities and stations in life. Paul greets slaves and masters, middle-class merchants, and at least one or two people of status and means. Among them are immigrants, Jews and Gentiles, and so on. By chapter's end, Paul has painted a strange and wonderful family portrait, with aristocrats and artisans, shopkeepers and slaves, men and women, Greeks and barbarians, worshipping together.

Those little Christian meetings changed the world. Nowhere else in the Roman Empire did people of all nations, religions, and classes gather in the same place, much less covenant to love one another—only in those earliest Christian living rooms. Clearly, the newborn church caught Jesus's habit of bringing people together across difference for a larger, common good. As Jesus prayed, God infused them with the unity that already existed between Creator and Redeemer. The contemporary American church needs to catch Jesus's habit, too, and our divided world needs us to have it. According to Jesus's prayer, that happens when Jesus is truly "in" us. And when that happens the world notices.

MISSION 4.0

Twenty centuries of Christians have broadly given the name "mission" to the way God calls us to love and have an impact on the world, and we have defined it variously. In contemporary Christianity, individual churches usually major in one or two of three ways to do mission.

Mission is evangelism, say some. And they are right. Jesus called us to "make disciples of all

nations" (Matthew 28:16–20), sent us to "be [his] witnesses in Jerusalem, Judea, Samaria and to the ends
of the earth" (Acts 1:8), and commissioned us to minister the "message of reconciliation" between God
and people (2 Corinthians 5:11–21). He also gave birth
to a church that came out of the womb proclaiming
the good news of a God who loves them and a Christ
who died for them (Acts 2:1–28:31). Christians share
Christ with their neighbors, invite them to church,
and reach out to them through Bible studies. Evangelism is Mission 1.0.

Mission is service, say others. And they are right.
John the Baptist told those with two cloaks or cans
of tuna to give one of them away to a neighbor without (Luke 3:11). In a powerful moment in the days
before his trial and death, Jesus called us to feed the
hungry, give drink to the thirsty, clothe the naked,
welcome the stranger, visit the sick and imprisoned
(Matthew 25:36–40). Christian churches build Habi-
tat for Humanity houses, serve at soup kitchens,
host job fairs for the unemployed, and build little
blue schoolhouses on the Mexican border; we serve.
And service is Mission 2.0.

Mission is advocacy, say still other Christians.
And they are right. John the Baptist called on people
in power, like tax collectors and soldiers, not to
extort their status inferiors (Luke 3:12–14). Mary cel-

ebrated and Jesus preached God's intention to raise the poor and the hungry from their lowly station and bring the rich down a peg (Luke 1:46–55; 6:20–21, 24–25). Jesus's Golden Rule ought to give people of privilege and power the imagination to know that, if powerless themselves, they would pine for someone to beseech the powerful on their behalf. In his notes for a sermon called "The One-Sided Approach to the Good Samaritan," Martin Luther King Jr., criticized the heroic helper, who "sought to soothe the effect of evil, without going back to its root causes."[6] To paraphrase King's point, "It's great that the Samaritan helped that poor guy, but we really gotta do something about all the people getting mugged on that road." Christians write to members of Congress, march in protests, and otherwise get on the nerves of the authorities, for Jesus. Advocacy is Mission 3.0.

To all three of these very different ways of understanding mission—evangelism, service, and advocacy—I say a loud "Amen!" We Christians have done our usual thing by dividing over which is *really* mission, but each is powerfully good. If you enthusiastically reach out to the world with the good news about Jesus (evangelism), some Christian will say you're presumptuously stepping on the toes of Jews, Muslims, and atheists. If you serve at a soup kitchen (service), another Christian will chide you for perpetuating the status quo. If you lobby passionately in the halls of government (advocacy), yet another Christian voice will say you're rearranging deck chairs on the *Titanic*, since Jesus is coming soon, and may quote, "The poor you will always have with you" (Matthew 26:11). We're human, so we try to find ways we're superior. But I say to evangelism and service and advocacy people, "Go, go, go, and do, and God bless you!"

This book exists to propose a fourth Christian mission: being one, as Jesus prayed. That seems strange at first, because unity seems more like an internal Christian thing than an outward-directed action. Churches who pay unity any attention at all usually delegate community-building to their fellowship committee. As we've seen, though, Jesus has one eye on the church and one on the world when he tells his disciples to "love one another as I have loved you" and prays for them and their disciples that "they all may be one" (John 13:34–35; 17:20–23). In those two moments and others, Jesus launches a Christian strategy for impact that no one seems to have recognized as mission: he says that when Christians love each other, it will change the world. People will know that we're Jesus people and know that God loves them here, not by our evangelism or our service or our advocacy, but by the way we love one another.

Thus, loving each other/being one with each other, too, is mission—call it Mission 4.0. This truth is both exhilarating and alarming. It thrills us, because truly faithful folk look for more ways to reach the world with God's love; it disquiets us because we have such a bad track record at this. We've seen throughout this book that Christians are infamous for being divided and divisive, and that we even pat ourselves on the back for it. We privilege right thinking and right acting—even right definition of mission—over our love for one another and our unity, so we squander a mission to which Jesus used his last earthly energy calling us.

Here's something we agree on: God loves the world and calls the church to join that love. As divided as American churches are from one another, it would be difficult to find one that couldn't sign on to God's love for the world and the church's call to love the world. We can build on that. Our twenty-first-century American cities, neighborhoods, states, and nations need help, friends. Deep and painful divisions have brought them to the brink of a cultural disaster. Families can't eat together, for fear of a political war breaking out around the table; urbanites can't talk to suburbanites and country people;

black people and white people are more at odds than they've been for a long while; our government leaders are stymied by partisan politics; the educated and the uneducated live in different worlds; and the economic classes are getting on one another's nerves. And no one is stepping up to lead them back to one another.

I nominate the Christian church for that job. We've seen in this book that the church seems at first a bad fit for the job, but God has a time-honored habit of hiring people who don't seem ready for the job. And in our time, true faithfulness to the one who prayed "that they all may be one . . . so that the world may know" almost requires it.

The saying goes that "God doesn't call the equipped, but rather equips the called." If Christians would learn and practice collaborating and building community across our differences, we could export that new skill and heal our land. The people of our city need someone to teach them how to find things they can do together well, how to stay in the same room when they disagree on important things, and how to talk to one another about those important things long enough to make something better than either person could have done alone. Loving our neighbor as ourselves and being faithful citizens of our nation may just require this ministry.

Jesus called us to love one another—even when we're different from one another. And he prayed that we would be one—even though we disagree. Paul pictured a church where a brilliant variety of gifts all move toward the common good (1 Corinthians 12:7). If that Jesus leads us and that Paul guides us, Christians could blaze the trail to a whole new world, where difference becomes an asset rather than a threat—a laboratory for a holy experiment that changes everything. It would be a good start for us to launch Meet through Mission projects together, even when we can't agree on anything but that. It would be great to start a Christian Mingle, so we know one another, build our muscles for a whole lot of blessed and Courageous Conversations,[7] and cultivate the enduring loyalty that comes from being different together over time.

SAVING THE WORLD

The time for redemptive Christian unity is now. We shouldn't need a natural disaster to bring us together. Jesus calls us to one another, and we've been wasting time. Consider the radical difference Christianity could have made in American culture if, a century ago, the Machen people and the Fosdick people had listened to Jesus's command, determined to become the answer to Jesus's prayer for unity, and stuck together. Imagine fundamentalists and liberals, conservative and progressive Christians learning in the same schools or worshipping in the same congregations and figuring out why God gave us one another. Or even if not worshipping in the same building, imagine them in the same town, coming together to understand one another and lead the nation to understand one another across the dividing lines of our strong convictions. Instead of two tribes warring over issues, we would have become two divinely formed parts of one joined community, with differently useful ways of seeing the world—all serving the common good together.

That constructive, enduring Christian collaboration across difference would then have shone into our wider culture to preempt some of its most damaging recent habits. Could we even fathom a corporation executive, a union boss, a law firm's partners, or a sports team owner saying, "My people are coming apart at the seams! I'd better go talk to those Christians. They seem to have a clue about community across difference." In a history-making oddity, universities, at a loss for how to conduct robust discussion across ideological distance, would have beaten a path straight to churches and seminaries for help. Government, too, would have looked to the

way our congregations and denominational sum-
mits tap disagreement to make something better.

Widen the aperture even further: imagine Christians had taken up unity as its mission from the
beginning. We could imagine earlier versions of
Christian community that would have helped us
avoid the sort of internal and external violence that
led to the Crusades and the Inquisitions. And now
look beyond Christianity. If Christians and
churches across the ages had built relationship with
our Abrahamic cousins, Judaism and Islam, our
habit of engagement would have informed those
relationships, too. Then interfaith conversations
would be reaching the crucial Left-Right divide in all
three religions. We can imagine a century of Christian, Jewish, and Muslim leaders challenging one
another to know and love not only one another but
their own religion's theological and political other
half. Then all three religions would be equipped to
save the world from its rampant division. What
would the world do in the face of such a community-
building force as religion would be?! We probably
wouldn't have seen the proliferation of books with
titles like Christopher Hitchens' *God Is Not Great:
How Religion Poisons Everything*. "The God of a group
that does that much good must be good." That's
what they might have said.

This is all retrospective fantasy. It would have been marvelous if the Christian church had come together across difference a century or even centuries ago; but we didn't stay together, after all, so we never learned the skills or got the experience to help our dangerously divided world.

Here's the good news: we can come together now. By God's grace, today, we have a choice. We can count our divisions inevitable and righteous, and so keep widening the aisle between our tribes; or we can imagine a new world, changed by a new Christian unity. If Christ's church wakes to the glories God has in store for those who stay engaged across our differences, maybe a century from now, someone will write a book chronicling the societal bridge that religion became in the twenty-first century.[8]

Against all odds, by God's grace, through God's Spirit, the church can save this divided world. In that hope, we would follow and channel Jesus, who loves to save the world. This courageous, countercultural move toward one another, this vision of becoming a true House United, is Mission 4.0, and the time to begin living into it is now.

Notes

1. The first citation of Mead's famous words is difficult to find, with experts imagining that she spoke it as an impromptu response to a question. Mead treats the power of small, committed groups most thoroughly in her *Continuities in Cultural Evolution* (New Haven: Yale University Press, 1964).

2. The quotation is from Meredith Cook, "What My Experience with Hurricane Harvey Taught Me about Missions," International Mission Board, August 31, 2017, http://tinyurl.com/ydfmg6yu. Examples of Christian collaboration in mission to Harvey abound. See J. A. Medders, "From the Flooded Grounds of Houston," Gospel Coalition, August 27, 2017, http://tinyurl.com/y725gcuv; Samaritan's Purse, "Samaritan's Purse Responds after Hurricane Harvey's Punch," August 28, 2017, http://tinyurl.com/yaykt5sa; Ed Stetzer, "Remember Teachings of Mr. Rogers and the Good Samaritan in Harvey Relief Efforts," *USA Today*, August 31, 2017, http://tinyurl.com/yb5ouhmq.

3. Dietrich Bonhoeffer, Letter of April 30, 1944.

4. Gerard Russell, *Heirs to Forgotten Kingdoms: Journeys into the Disappearing Religions of the Middle East* (New York: Basic, 2014).

5. See chapter 4 above, where a klatch of progressive Christians try to fathom why 81 percent of white evangelicals voted for Donald Trump. Their answers make it clear that they don't know any evangelicals personally.

6. Martin Luther King Jr., "The One-Sided Approach of the Good Samaritan," November 20, 1955, The Martin Luther King, Jr. Papers Project, Standford, PDF, https://tinyurl.com/ycleeqvh.

7. Courageous Conversations and Christian Mingle are capitalized here, because they are specific ministries that I and others help lead through House United in local churches, schools, universities, seminaries, civic groups, etc. For materials and coaching, check out www.house unitedmovement.org.

8. Through my work with House United these days, I plant seeds for Courageous Conversation in churches across the nation. We've done charged engagement on gun control and the existence of the devil (later in Wayzata); civil but animated discussion about gay marriage for congregation leaders (Greens Farms Church in Westport, Connecticut, and Manhattan Beach Community Church, California); controlled rumbles on whether the United States is a Christian nation, how free speech should be, what is the proper role of church and state in assisting the poor, immigration, and health

care (Pinnacle Presbyterians in Scottsdale, Arizona); and other hot topics that have flowed out of this work at Avon Lake UCC outside Cleveland, First-Plymouth UCC in Lincoln, Manhattan Beach Community Church in So Cal, and others.

Next, we'll take Courageous Conversations (House United–style) to denominations and academe, two idea-based communities having trouble with their differences. I've already hosted one at a Presbytery gathering within the Presbyterian Church (USA) in Phoenix, Arizona; co-led a United Methodist conference gathering in Indiana; and brought UCC pastors into controversial conversation in their annual Conversations conference. Since academic leaders see that changing policy doesn't usually change culture, they've begun to ask for help with conversations, too. All of this means that you should watch for Courageous Conversations "Coming Soon to a Church or School Near You." When we bring our differences into play with an eye for the advantage they offer, God does good things . . . and smiles.

Acknowledgments

Finishing this book leaves me humbled and grateful. I thank Tony Jones and Layne Johnson at Fortress Press for their patience and support; John Ross and the congregation of Wayzata Community Church for embodying an extraordinarily inclusive way of being church; Wes Avram and Pinnacle Presbyterian Church for hosting courageous experiments; and a host of other church, seminary, and business leaders who have embraced the vision of this book and let me come alongside them to help build communities across difference. Above all I'm grateful to Liz, Sam, and Isaac, for freeing me to write, bolstering my spirit, and making our home a house united.